Harry Greene's
WEEKEND DIY
Painting &
Decorating

First published in 2006 by
Lawpack Publishing Limited
76–89 Alscot Road
London SE1 3AW
www.lawpack.co.uk

Text and line drawings © 2006 Harry Greene
Design © 2006 Lawpack Publishing Limited

For details of photograph copyright owners see Acknowledgements page

ISBN 1 905261 18 7

Printed in Great Britain

Contents

Acknowledgements

The author and publisher would like to thank the following for their generous help in making available product photographs for reproduction in this book.

Page number and position (r = right, l = left, t = top, c = centre, b = bottom)

Aston Trading Ltd 37, 38

Clear Group 42

Crown Paints 22, 24t, 24b, 26

H&R Johnson Tiles 66c, 66r, 67 all, 68, 69t, 69b, 72b

Imperial Home Decor 54

L G Harris & Co Ltd 20b, 34 all, 36, 51 all, 56, 62b

RMC Specialist Products 19, 20t, 31

SK Enterprises 7

Cover photograph of Harry Greene by Andrew Edgecumbe

All other photographs © Harry Greene

Introduction

Myths have grown up surrounding the techniques of painting and decorating, both of which are really fairly easy to master. So I want to give you heart and convince you that with all the new wonderful materials and innovative tools available, and with application and determination, you have all that you need to begin.

Do you realise that you have completed at least 50 per cent of the work of redecorating a room when the preparation work is completed? It might be a bit of hard physical work, but it's not beyond an enthusiastic DIYer's ability. The apparent tedium of preparation (or preparing the substrate as the professionals call it) is not to be exaggerated, but there is no short cut to the success of this most rewarding of DIY jobs. I have often said that the most satisfying DIY jobs are those where material costs are low but labour charges could be very high. Decorating is a fine example of one of these jobs. To convince you to make a start, think of this: of the total cost of redecorating a room, only 20 per cent of the total cost is chargeable to materials. The rest is attributable to labour charges. For example, redecorating a small bedroom at, say, a total cost of £400 means 20 per cent for the materials, or £80. You'll save £320 by doing it yourself. Decorating is therefore a DIY task in which you can save a lot of money. It is also very satisfying. Mind, it will take longer than a professional, but then we DIYers have time on our side!

Harry Greene

Painting

Preparation
Planning

Pay particular attention to the planning and preparation stages. Before rushing out to buy a pot of paint, relax, sit down with a pen and paper and begin to note

80 per cent of a painting job is labour, so buy the best and do-it-yourself!

all the preliminaries. You might feel that you don't know enough to even begin, but read on. You're about to begin the first and very important part of the job. Do it properly and in the end you'll have a finished decorating job that you'll be proud of.

A few notes and queries for you to jot down at this point are as follows:

1. Surfaces must be clean and dry (this can mean and lot scraping and sanding). Household dirt is mostly silica and carbon found as a coat of grease. Often it is indiscernible but it prevents paint adhering properly! All you need to do to get rid of the grease is to prepare the surface by thoroughly cleaning it with an ordinary household cleaning agent.

2. If there is a chimney, maybe have it swept before you start?

3. Is there ingress of rainwater anywhere, maybe from a cracked window sill or from a gap between the window frame and the brick window reveal? Is putty cracked on the lower edge of a window allowing water to seep in?

4. It is worth stripping all self-adhesive foam insulation from doors and windows. It attracts dirt and grime.

5. Wipe off the tops of doors and window frames where a layer of dirt can hide, otherwise you could find grey streaks of dirt in your bright new paint.

6 Vacuum dust out from keyholes and around window latches (another source of grey streaks in paint). Dust, of course, is the enemy of the painter: not only does it leave grey streaks but a gritty surface too. Another enemy is damp. Never ever paint a damp surface or wood that has a high moisture content.

7 If you have been told to strip all paint from a surface before redecorating (or just think that you have to), then you could be wasting a lot of time. Yes, you do have to make sure that the surface is properly prepared, but if the paint is sound, tough and smooth (with no flaking or cracking) then all you need is a piece of sandpaper. What you have to do is to 'key' the surface. A build up of paint layers on the edge of a door or window can often cause it to stick. This occurs usually on the hinge edge of the door when the brush has been overloaded and wiped down the face of the door to leave a build up on the edge of the stile.

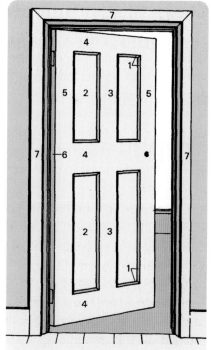

Painting a panelled door
After the preparation, allow plenty of time to paint a panelled door. Allow plenty of time for the edges to dry properly before shutting a door. Paint the beads and panels first, then follow the order as shown so that the natural joins will be invisible. Leave the handle edge to last so it is easier to open and close the door whilst you are working on it.

8 A useful tip, before you start painting, is to make certain that you can get a coin into the gap between the door and the frame. If you can't, use a paint scraper to remove the build up of paint. Then you'll have to start as if for new wood. If paint is chipped, flaking or cracked, remove it and any loose surrounding paint.

9 When only a thin film of paint has to be removed, one easy and effective method to solve the problem is to use an orbital sander with a fine grit paper. Wear a mask and goggles for this dusty job, even if the machine might have a vacuum dust extractor. Always use a rag dipped in white spirit to remove residual dust before applying paint.

Chemical paint strippers

Liquid paint strippers are difficult to apply to a vertical surface and will sometimes run down forming rivers which could show through the repainted surface. A thick jelly type stripper is best for vertical surfaces. Use it only where necessary and take careful note of the instructions. Use gloves and protect your eyes and nose. Don't forget to protect the floor: old newspapers are best as they are easily disposed of. When you see the paint shrivelling after applying the liquid paint stripper, remove it with a flat steel painter's scraper. A filling knife looks similar but is too flexible for this job. You'll soon get the hang of it, but do allow the

Different methods of stripping paint depend on area, flat or moulded, vertical or horizontal. A new paste stripper takes off seven coats in one go and leaves the wood almost as new – as this door testifies!

stripper time to work. Get rid of the debris by folding it into the newspapers. Tie them up and then dispose of them in a plastic bag.

Painting old wooden windows

These need a lot of careful preparation. If the original paint is sound there is no need to strip it, but you do need to 'key' it by gently sanding with a fine gauge paper. Replace perished putty and take off the stay and handle. It is easier to paint a small casement window when it has been unscrewed. Check for open joints and rotted end grain. Use a wood-hardener if necessary. Paint in the order indicated in the drawing.

Finish off, after again checking the instructions and the expected result, by rubbing over the surface with medium steel wool. The wood will suck the liquid stripper beneath the surface, so you'll need to neutralise it before applying paint. The instructions on the tin will tell you which solvent to use otherwise use white spirit on a clean lint-free rag to rub over the entire surface. When stripping paint from door mouldings, you'll need to use a shave-hook. These are inexpensive flat pieces of metal with a wooden handle. A heart-shaped scraper will deal with all the mouldings on doors, but apply two or three layers of stripper, then the wood will be revealed more easily. Use a metal container, pouring in a little of the stripper. Brush it on liberally. It will shrivel quite quickly, then apply another coat. Protect your hands and eyes and provide added ventilation if working inside. A test on a small area will tell you how much you need to apply, how long it needs to react with the paint and whether you need to use the scraper between successive coats of the stripper.

> **Paint skin in old paint will never mix in – strain the leftover paint through old tights.**

Heat gun

A heat gun is a marvellous tool for removing large flat areas of paint. Buy one with a reputable brand name because a power tool needs to have a guarantee. Obviously where the heat is the source of energy you'll need to take a certain amount of care, but, as with many power tools, these are easier to use than most people think. Around the area where you intend to work, remove curtains and inflammable materials even though there is no actual flame round the gun. There are usually two levels of heat controlled with a rotor switch. Keep the trailing flex safely to one side and, if you stop, switch off the power. Try it out in a hidden area or on a scrap of painted wood to get used to handling the gun and the scraper. Don't scrape up into the hot loosened paint, it could fall on to your hands. You'll actually be amazed how easy it is to loosen the paint and to see it melt, but keep moving the gun so as not to scorch any wood surfaces that have been bared.

Paint stripping
Use a cordless hot air gun to strip large areas of paint. Scrape with a stripping knife, not with a filling knife. Wear gloves.

Some guns come with a built-in scraper and other accessories. You'll be told in the instructions to hold the scraper at an angle so that the hot paint falls to the floor. Make sure not to use newspapers on the floor! Use a sheet of non-combustible board instead. You must have protection from the fumes which will be generated and open a window to get plenty of ventilation. Eyes and skin too can be vulnerable, so again, please wear protection!

> **Sugar soap removes grime and grease from painted surfaces.**

Abrasive papers

One of the irritating aspects of burning-off paint is clogging. To solve this problem, apply a solution of garden-lime and water to the painted area some time before using the heat gun. To complete the stripping process, use, as the instructions indicate, different grades of glasspaper, wire wool or wet-and-dry paper (silicone carbide paper: wetted as you might use it on cars). You should be able to judge just how much 'smoothing' the stripped surface needs by rubbing the palm of your hand over it. If any of the grain (wood fibre) has lifted, it will be necessary to use a medium glasspaper first to get a smooth surface before finally smoothing it like glass with a finer paper. The best results on large areas are obtained by rubbing with a strip of abrasive paper wrapped over a block of wood or a specially formed cork block (available at all DIY stores). Usually, glasspaper comes in three types – coarse, medium and fine – but in the trade code numbers are used to order intermediate types. The lower numbers show coarser grades (or 'grits') than the higher numbers. Yellow glasspaper is the most common type and has different grits, either closely packed to produce a fine finish or widely spaced to do two things – reduce clogging and to take off more surface. If you are working on oak or other hardwoods, you'll need to order garnet abrasive paper. This deals with hardwoods quite easily because it does not shed its grits as quickly as glasspaper and only comes in the finer grades. However, silicone carbide wet-and-dry paper gives the smoothest of all finishes, especially on oak, beech, birch and other hardwoods.

Pigment and medium separate in paints, so stir gently to blend them.

New wood

Try this as an experiment. Wet your finger and touch some new wood. You'll find that the moisture is readily absorbed into the wood so sealing is the first step in the preparation work. A priming coat of paint provides this essential seal base, so that the undercoat (and gloss or top coat) is not sucked into the wood. The primer must be worked well into the grainy surface and the wood totally covered in an evenly applied coat. The priming coat also acts as an inhibitor to damp and moisture. This is why

Follow instructions when painting new wood. Preparation, properly carried out, ensures success. Don't skimp on materials and always use good brushes. Sand the surface between coats and allow plenty of drying time. Cover a third of the bristles and brush from dry to wet when 'laying off'.

it is important to paint the back and front of wood to be newly fixed, like skirting boards and architraves. Don't be tempted under any circumstances to use the lazy person's method of priming, that is, with emulsion paint. It is water-based and therefore dries quickly but is not compatible with oil-based paints and does not offer the protection of a priming coat.

Use floor and furniture coverings and dust sheets to protect the surrounding area. It's good practice to transfer paint from the tin into a smaller paint 'kettle'. Tie a piece of string across the paint kettle from handle to handle, and wipe off any excess paint from the brush. Another tip – dip only a third of the length of the bristles into the paint, any deeper and you'll find it running back down the handle as you paint.

Application

When you think about it, what we're really doing when we are painting is providing an enhanced, overall surface effect on wood and protecting its surface at the same time. We are forming a

Paint a front door only after removing the handle, knocker, letterbox, etc.

continuous surface film on the wood. Only by following correct procedures is it possible to build up a good, hard wearing and easy-to-clean surface. After the priming coat is dry and hard, sand it to obtain a smooth surface. Wipe off residual dust with a cloth dipped in white spirit. The next layer of a conventional painting job on new wood is the undercoat, sometimes called the obliterating coat. This is because it gives a good 'cover'. This coat has 'body' and helps build up the paint film. When you take a brush loaded with paint to the wood, it has to end up evenly spread with no runs and no apparent joins. To achieve this, spread the paint in the direction of the grain and then lightly across it at right angles.

Finally, working from the adjacent (unpainted) area, stroke back into the painted area very lightly, lifting the brush off after each even stroke. This is called 'laying off' and is the solution to irritating blobs, thinly spread paint and runs. Never put the brush into the wet area to draw it along to the area where fresh paint is to be next applied. Let the undercoat dry thoroughly.

Get help with the next stage, which can be very satisfying but laborious! Ask anybody, with the energy to spare, to lightly sand over the whole painted area. To get an even surface use someone with a gentle touch so that the same pressure is applied. Avoid too much exertion. A fine abrasive paper is all that is necessary, but to get the top coat with a mirror finish that looks professional, it is essential to get the undercoat beautifully smooth. I cannot overemphasise the importance of this stage. A final smoothing with wet-and-dry paper will get the desired finish. The paper should be kept just damp and use a cork sanding block. A fine residue is always produced but is easily washed off. Remember, use a dampened cloth with white spirit to give a pleasing undercoat job.

The top coat of paint must be applied in the same way as the undercoat, always working in the direction of the grain to start with. After the final brush strokes have laid off the finished coat, make sure that there are no residual brush marks. Slight variations in the paint application should flow out as the paint dries. Don't ever be tempted to go back on to the work after it has become tacky, you'll end up with an awful mess. But don't despair, if you're not too happy with your first results you can always go back when it is dry. If that's the case give it a good rub down and start again. Of course, this time you won't need to apply a priming coat, just another coat of gloss, but do make absolutely sure that you've smoothed the surface properly before any application of paint.

Sometimes new wood will have been prepared with a preservative before reaching the merchant. If you know, or suspect, this is the case and you want to paint it, the solution is aluminium wood primer. There are some 'don'ts' though. For example, never use it on hardwood such as teak, which has a greasy surface. You'll need to degrease this with white spirit first. Allow it to dry thoroughly.

Manufacturers' instructions on paint tins are the result of their own research and must be followed. Different paint brands are not

It is easier to remove spilled paint by first covering it with sand or earth.

necessarily compatible and the unsuited chemical constituents might give a lot of problems if you try to mix them, so stick to the same brand of primer, undercoat and top coat. Adhesion may

Before opening a can of paint, wipe the lid to stop dirt falling inside.

be compromised, as may be the flexing and contraction properties of each coat under different weather conditions. This could result in flaking, blistering and cracking. Check with your paint supplier, who will tell you about the new paints on the market. For example, if you're not interested in a conventional approach to painting, there are paints that have two coats in one. This is obviously a quicker method of painting, but because of the texture of the paint it is sometimes more difficult to obtain an absolutely mirror-like finish. Other paints like acrylic resin-based paints are very flexible and will move with the expansion and contraction of wood. This will prevent the problems of cracking and peeling if the paint is exposed to the weather. Two other positive factors are that they are very easy to apply and you simply wash out brushes (and your hands) under the tap.

Problems

Runs and rivers

It is not always possible to see runs and rivers forming on a vertical surface when painting in bad light. Even if you've correctly applied the paint with not too much on the brush, unless it is evenly distributed runs can occur and it's only when the paint is dry that these runs and rivers show up badly especially in a side light. They can also occur if the brush is unwittingly overloaded or if not enough time is taken to 'lay off' the paint by drawing the brush back into the wet paint from the last application or the 'dry' area. Patience is a virtue in relation to painting finishing techniques. You should only try to remove unsightly runs when they are dry. If they are showing up heavily, use a jelly paint stripper and start again as from new wood. Fine runs can be gently removed with a medium to fine glasspaper. Try to 'feather edge' the runs into the surrounding paint until you are unable to feel any ridges with your finger, then you'll only need a top coat to complete the task.

Blisters

There are a number of reasons why blisters appear on a painted surface, depending on the substrate (what's underneath) or the type of paint used. Emulsion paint, for example, used on an oil-based painted wall which was not properly prepared for emulsion paint, results in blisters appearing. These can also result by painting on a damp wall. A wall has to be thoroughly dry to prevent them. If necessary, hire a dehumidifier, especially if a room has been replastered. A wall has to be firm, flat and degreased. A stabilising primer should be used to bind powdery or flaking plaster wall surfaces.

Blisters on a painted wooden surface can be caused by painting on to damp wood or by knots that do not have a shellac coating to prevent the resin pushing up the layer of paint. Use an aluminium primer before painting. Resin can break out in new wood anywhere along the grain, so check thoroughly before applying any primer. When carrying out the initial sanding, a sticky patch will certainly indicate resin escaping and will need sealing.

Dimpled paint

Condensation or any dampness in the air when painting can cause this irritating problem, so make sure the room is well ventilated whilst you are painting. If condensation forms as the paint dries – most often this can be seen on oil-based paints – it may be that warm moist air from a boiling kettle or from cooking has come into contact with the colder surface that you are painting.

Another reason for dimpled paint is that the surface being painted has not been prepared properly. All surfaces must be firm with no friable, powdery surfaces and absolutely clean and degreased, and keyed ready to receive the paint.

Pitting

There are rules that have to be followed when painting any surface with any paint. Nothing can be left to chance. Recommended procedures are important to avoid common problems. A common mistake is trying to paint when rain is imminent. The tiniest raindrops on fresh paint will result in a surface pitted with unsightly marks. This also happens if damp air indoors becomes atomised from a steaming kettle or something similar. If it has occurred and you have the problem, let it dry completely before rubbing down with fine glasspaper until you have an absolutely smooth surface, one where you cannot feel anything but a mirror-like finish beneath the tips of your fingers. Clean off the residue with a rag and white spirit, allow to dry thoroughly and then apply a new top coat under proper painting conditions.

Flaking

Moisture will cause lack of adhesion, resulting in the paint lifting off and flaking. This can occur after painting if moisture has been allowed to continue its migration to the wall surface. Other reasons for flaking paint are (a) painting on to a damp or contaminated surface, (b) applying emulsion over a glossed painted wall and (c) painting on to a powdery surface. If flaking has occurred, strip off all loose and flaking paint and thoroughly sand the wall back to a stable substrate. Clean off, allow the wall to dry and apply a coat of primer sealer, obtainable from all suppliers. Exterior painted wood with a flaking surface is unsightly and the direct result of poor preparation. If the timber has not been allowed to dry out before

Flaking interior paint

If the paint on an interior surface has 'flaked' or blistered, remove all signs of the loose material. Fill, level and allow to dry. Then apply a coat of stabilising liquid or diluted PVA adhesive with a roller to give a base for the final finish.

being painted, the moisture will try to escape when the summer sun warms up the wood. Sometimes shoddily prepared timber will have been given a coat of emulsion before a top coat of gloss. This will not last a season and flaking is bound to occur. Remove all traces of unsound paint and allow the wood to dry thoroughly. Only when the wood is absolutely dry can you start the preparation work for recoating. Use a medium grit sandpaper to feather edge the edges of the solid paint that is left, then proceed with a primer, undercoat and top coat. I am sure that you are now fully aware of how important it is to observe the drying time, the sanding and the cleaning for each successive coat.

Crazing

A painted surface appears to have been done professionally with no apparent blemishes or faults, but if a top coat of an oil-

Clean a wall to be painted, from the bottom up, to avoid 'runs' on the dirty wall.

based paint has been applied to an undercoat that was not completely dry and hard, crazing will result (we are not talking here of crazing intentionally carried out on, for example, antique furniture or reproduction furniture). You can also find it happening on surfaces that had not been properly rinsed of any chemical cleaning material. To solve the problem there's no alternative but to rub down with wet-and-dry paper when the paint is dry in preparation for an application of fresh paint. However, if the crazing is deep and you don't want to remove the paint or varnish over a large area, there is an alternative. Simply use a proprietary brand of filler, smoothed over the entire surface with a hard plastic spatula or float. Once it is dry, use the finest grit glasspaper to get a mirror-like finish. Then go through the painting processes as before.

Efflorescence

This is a white deposit of salts found on surfaces of plaster, concrete, brick or stone. It is caused by alkaline salts, naturally found in the building materials, being brought to the surface in the drying out process. It is often seen on the brickwork of new houses, where in time it disappears when all the salts have migrated to the surface. Never be tempted to wash off the salts with a liquid cleaner or with vinegar – a Victorian idea! This will only compound the problem and not solve it. Simply rub off the white deposit with sacking, and keep doing it until no more appears – it's

Painting walls

'Cross'-paint walls with emulsion paint two or three times. This spreads the paint evenly. Do the same with stabilising solution, which is best applied with a roller.

Just brush off powder on walls, these salts will eventually dry out.

Painting window frames

Use masking tape to prevent paint from spreading onto glass, but leave 2 mm (1/16 in) so that the paint can make a seal between it and the wooden window frame.

got to end some time! If it occurs on an indoor wall, hire a dehumidifier to help the drying out process. This will help speed up the 'bringing-to-the-surface' of the salts. Once the wall has dried out, clean off completely and, if you want to decorate, apply an alkali-resistant primer first. Follow the manufacturer's instructions exactly and then redecorate as you had planned.

Walls

Even newly built or newly surfaced walls will need a certain amount of preparation before paint can be applied. Older walls and those that are uneven or cracked will need even

A wall with blemishes needs a matt finish, gloss will highlight the high spots.

more! However, whatever preparation work has to be done, safety and a proper foundation for your choice of wall finish are the most important considerations at this stage. If ladders or stepladders are to be used, get to know how to handle and stabilise them. Stepladders should always have the feet against the skirting board. If you place them parallel to the wall any slight pressure on a drill or even a scraper can tilt the ladder away from the wall and cause a fall. Ladders should be erected at the correct angle, that is for every 1200 mm (4 ft) up the wall the feet should be 300 mm (1 ft) out from the wall. Stepladders are best with good wide flat rungs, so one doesn't get too tired standing on one for long periods. A clip-on tray or a fixed, folding platform to hold paint kettles and tools is a bonus.

Cracks

A crack in a plastered wall will need to be raked out and given a key shape by widening the crack at its deepest point, so that when filler is forced into the crack, it becomes its own anchor when dry by forming a wedge shape. Filler can be mixed with emulsion paint if that is to be the wall coating. In

Cover cracks between walls and ceilings with easily fixed coving.

this way, the crack repair will absorb the emulsion paint at the same rate as the surrounding wall and not show up as a dried repair. When the repair is drying, smooth and feather edge it with a dampened paintbrush. When completely dry use a block with wet-and-dry glasspaper wrapped around it to get an invisible repair. If the crack is deep and wide you'll need to reinforce the repair with a fine net tape but back-fill the crack first before bedding the tape into the filler and use a wide plastic float to get an even finish with a feather edge. If the crack is worryingly deep, check that the wall is not a 23 cm (9 in) wall with a corresponding crack on the outside of the brickwork. If this is the case, you'll need to get professional advice. It could be that this has been caused by subsidence underneath the foundations.

Uneven surfaces

If a plastered wall is to be redecorated but has an uneven surface, solve the problem by smoothing out the bumps and filling in the hollows. Alternatively resurface the whole wall with plasterboard – this is termed dry-lining. To carry out the former, a tub of one-coat plaster is best for the hollows, but first of all hold a long straight-edged batten horizontally and vertically against the wall at different levels, so that you can mark the hollows and the bumps. Use a scraper to get rid of the biggest bumps, finishing off with a sanding machine. Wear protective clothing and personal protection against the dust. Also, either keep windows open or, if the room is empty, seal around the door with masking tape to stop dust getting through the door cracks. Once you've got rid of any bumps, the rest is relatively easy. The premixed plaster is easily spread and levelled with a small straight batten before smoothing it with your plastic float. Before applying the plaster in small lumps with a filling knife, dampen the whole area. Finish off each repair very gently smoothing the plaster with a wet paintbrush. You might need a second coat, when the first is dry, to fill any

Using the incredible paint stick, it is possible to paint 6 sq m (64 sq ft) of wall space in under 5 minutes. The transparent hollow handle has a suction action to hold the paint, and comes with an adaptor to fit any container.

misses. Finally, a coat of plasticiser or diluted PVA will give you a great levelled wall ready for decorating.

Dry-lining

If you decide that the wall needs a completely new surface and you have room to lose 50 mm (2 in) off the length of the room, dry-lining is the solution. This is simply battening out the wall to receive plasterboards or a decorative panelled wall finish like tongue and grooved boards, or even laminated boards of simulated wood grain pattern. You have to take into account windows and doors to get good corner joints, also electric power points and switches have to be brought forward for safe fixing to the new wall surface. Another method of fixing the plasterboards to the wall is by using blobs of plaster. You have to decide whether or not you are going to remove the skirting boards and replace them on top of the new plasterboard surface. If not, cut the plasterboard to fit tightly against one of the side walls. If coving exists, the plasterboard will fit tightly to it and discrepancies can be filled with plaster later. With blobs about every 450 mm (18 in) apart, press the board firmly into the blobs of plaster and support it until it is dry. Turn off the supply to any circuit that supplies a socket or a switch which you intend to bring forward. You should find plenty of slack in the wiring to be able to bring the switch forward by 25 mm (1 in). Accurately cut the squared holes in the plasterboard and by using longer holding screws through the switch plate, you should be able to safely tighten up the switch plate to the new plasterboard surface. Switch back on at the mains to check. Joints around the plasterboards and the butted vertical joints can be filled with plaster and smoothed ready for decorating. A coat of plasticiser or diluted PVA is a good idea to help seal the new plaster wall and prepare it for decorating.

Stabilising

There are various methods of treating walls before beginning the redecorating stage. It depends on the substrate (what the wall is under the finish), what condition the surface is in and what the wall has been coated with previously. Brickwork that has been stripped of plaster to reveal the original bonding and mortar courses will need to be sealed to bind the border to prevent it becoming powdery. At the same time, the bricks will benefit from a coating of stabilising primer. If an attractive brick wall has

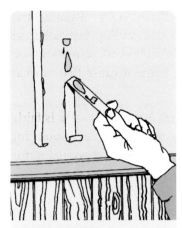

Stabilising walls

If you suspect that there might be old distemper on a wall or ceiling, you must remove it before redecorating. Use clear adhesive tape to test for distemper (which is powdered chalk and diluted glue). If the surface comes off in flakes it is likely to be distemper. Warm water and lots of elbow-grease will remove it. Apply a stabilising solution to seal the surface.

been exposed for aesthetic reasons and you've decided to leave it as part of the decor with a coat of paint, prime it with a stabilising primer as the base coat. A general purpose stabilising solution can be made by diluting a PVA bonding agent with water, but do not confuse it with stabilising primer which is specially formulated for powdery surfaces only. It will bond flaky wall surfaces but it is advisable to scrape off as much loose material as possible without disturbing the stable surrounding area. Fill the small indentations with a proprietary plaster filler, which should be a quick drying one, so you'll not be held up on the preparatory part of the work.

You can get information leaflets from your DIY store or a builders' merchant on all the available primers and sealers. Find one that is going to suit your particular repair job. A general purpose primer will give you sufficient sealing properties for porous walls and if you have an area on a wall that has lost its protective coating and is now patchy, it will provide the base for your chosen finish. It is suitable for solid walls and chipboard, hardboard and plywood walls. An alkali-resistant primer can be used very effectively on walls of brick, plaster, stone, concrete, render and absorbent fibre boards. This type of primer will give protection to oil-based paints, should any of the above have an alkali content, which could have an adverse effect on the paint if it were not protected.

Finishes

Think of paint as a film covering a hard surface, which will provide protection as well as a decorative finish to suit your personal taste. The film of paint covering a wall provides protection against general wear and tear and should be durable enough to last years, or until your creativity

Paint pads can be used successfully on all surfaces, inside and out. Here a stippled exterior wall is being painted with just one application.

demands a different colour. Painting and decorating is a rewarding experience so don't be afraid to express your own taste in your own home because that is what it's all about!

Choosing paint for interior walls is fairly easy; usually we choose emulsion for ceilings and walls and gloss paint for woodwork. Emulsion paint is water-based, so thin it with water if you need and wash brushes and your hands in water too. Emulsion paint does have a constituent, a vinyl or acrylic, which makes it tougher when dry. The choice of finish is personal too, be it matt (a dull finish with no sheen), eggshell, silk, satin or whole gloss.

Follow the manufacturer's instructions carefully, especially if you choose a thixotropic (jelly-like) or a microscopic (moisture permeable for new plaster) paint. What they don't tell you anywhere on the label is how to paint over old distemper (the old-fashioned whitewash used up until the 1950s). It was not a good covering because it came off on your hands when the wall became wet. The mix was simply powdered chalk, glue and water, so no wonder it had no lasting quality. If you do have to solve that problem on a wall, scrape off flakes, brush off loose material and apply a specially formulated stabilising primer which comes in clear or white. Then you can safely paint the wall with no trace of the original covering.

Victorian decoration in a hall often included a dado rail (chair back protection) and a heavily embossed wallpaper between it and the high

Paint pads and rollers are quicker to use than emulsion brushes.

skirting board. This attractive feature is being restored in many houses of that age by DIYers to give an authentic feel to period property. The embossed wallpapers were often painted with oil paint, which gave a lovely gloss finish and extra protection at the same time. However, the surface of your wall must be very flat before you attempt to give it a coat of gloss paint. Any cracks, not properly levelled, and uneven surfaces will show up. Working by artificial light is much more difficult, so if you're planning to redecorate a room, schedule it for the weekend, so that you get as much daylight as possible. Buy the best tools and materials that you can afford.

Emulsion paint

Painting walls with emulsion paint is easier and quicker with a roller or a pad. Kits are available for both. Paint rollers come in different forms and paint sticks hold sufficient paint in the long hollow handle to paint 6 sq m (64 sq ft). It takes only 5 minutes to comfortably cover that area – a great innovative idea. Other rollers in kit form have the paint actually poured into the roller itself, so there is no stopping to climb down a stepladder to dip into a paint tray.

Paint pads in kit form are now as popular as rollers were when they were first introduced to DIYers years ago. A large pad, about 200 mm by 75 mm (8 in by 3 in) covers evenly with none of the effort needed to wield an emulsion brush. Smaller pads are used for cutting in to frames and around switches. There are even triangular shaped pads to ensure that walls meeting at a corner are not left with misses. The pad kit comes with a narrow deep tray with a built-in roller that dispenses the paint evenly on to the pad. Other innovative ideas are the extension handle for getting to the tops of high walls without having to use a stepladder and curved pads to fit cornices and coving.

To paint narrow walls without getting joins and misses, start at the corner with a neat line up to the adjacent wall. Continue the line for about a metre (a yard) along the ceiling and the skirting board. Fill in that strip. Filling in is the fun part because you get immediate results. Now work in metre length strips along the wall vertically. Unless you have a cove or cornice between the wall and the ceiling, you'll find that most plastered walls at the ceiling joint are not exactly straight. It may only be a slight indent or just a bit uneven, but your job is to make it look straight. The best way, to avoid emphasising an uneven join, is to keep the wall colour at the lowest part of the join and in a straight line. Never let the wall colour creep on to the ceiling and never paint a straight line actually in the whole of the join even though you think it's absolutely straight. It really will show up badly after the paint has dried. For a wider room, work right round the walls in horizontal bands. Standard emulsion paints will need two coats. However, there are one-coat emulsion paints on the market that are more opaque than the standard type. This high-opacity emulsion paint must not be spread too thinly, otherwise you'll defeat the purpose of using it, that is to save time and to get density in one coat.

Ceilings

Always paint ceilings first if you are decorating a room completely. If you decide to use a roller, you will still have to use a small brush to paint round the edges first. However, pads have a plastic edge which gives a straight tight finish around the edge of the ceiling. There is no strong argument for using a roller or a pad because both can come with extended handles that can be used without the need to climb a stepladder. Safety must be a prime consideration when painting a ceiling. If you work from a plank or platform make certain it's safe and stable, and place it so that you don't have to change its position too often. Wear protective clothing because

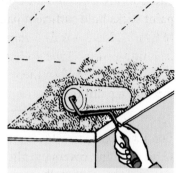

Mentally divide a ceiling into square metre (square yard) areas for painting. Paint in 'bands' across the areas so that joins are not visible.

rollers can spatter paint even when you take great care. Don't worry about the ceiling looking patchy as you roll as long as you roll back and forth and criss-cross to even up the paint. You might be alarmed at how the paint is drying but within a short time the painted ceiling will look flat and even. Emulsion paint has that quality. Remember whether you've chosen a paint that is meant for two coats or a more opaque one-coat paint. Follow the manufacturer's instructions.

You can start painting the ceiling in a corner but you have to work out the direction of the first 600 mm (2 ft) band

A new elite system for decorating ceilings has been developed based on a coating, which is then cleverly patterned with an incised roller. The edging also has a matching coving, easily cut and applied with fibrous plaster adhesive.

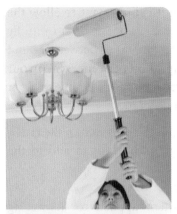

High ceilings give some DIY decorators excuses to skip the preparation work. Cleaning and applying stabilising solution or rolling emulsion is easy with a long-handled roller!

by deciding which way the light from the window falls. You should work away from the light. Try to blend in all joins and meeting areas so that there are no misses. The only fitting to paint around will be a light rose. These are usually the type that have a cover to unscrew to get to the terminal block and wiring. It is easily accessible but the first thing to do is to switch off at the mains and tape over the switch, or if the circuit has a removable fuse, take it out and keep it in your pocket until the job is finished. This, of course, means that you have to work in daylight, so start the job early on in the day. After unscrewing the ceiling rose let it slip down the light cable to rest against the bulb holder (after removal of the light shade). When the cover is rescrewed it will cover any blemishes and have a professional clean finish. Once the base coat is completed, you can use any paint technique covered in this section to give a special effect.

Furniture

A great deal of furniture is purchased in kit form for you to assemble. It is usually unpainted but has been sealed with a primer. If you choose to paint it, assemble it first with the screws and bolts fairly loose. Leave it for a while to acclimatise to the ambient temperature of the house. This is for a good reason. Primer or a first spray coat seal is not good enough to protect the furniture from moisture. As a consequence it will have been subjected to moisture at the factory, at the store and in transit. This causes the individual parts of the wood to swell. If different woods

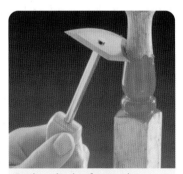

For hundreds of years the classic-shaped 'shavehook' has been used to remove paint from flat areas and particularly curved surfaces such as spindles and chair legs.

have been used they will react differently, so it is important to allow the furniture to shrink as the warm atmosphere dries it out. In a centrally heated home, timber normally has a moisture content of between 12 and 20 per cent. Some timbers in transit have up to 35 per cent. When your assembled piece of furniture has been in your home for a couple of days, tighten up all the fixings and you're ready to decorate.

Gently rub down the surface with glasspaper in the direction of the grain. Dampen it very slightly only to raise the grain, but not to add to the moisture content. Then use a sanding block with fine glasspaper to get a mirror-like finish to take your primer which will be compatible with the top coat. Patience is certainly a virtue when applied to decorating furniture. It cannot be rushed. Whether you are painting a kitchen chair, a chest of drawers or a wardrobe, there has to be a step-by-step procedure to follow. So think carefully. The techniques that can be applied after you've painted a finished top coat will be covered next in this section.

Both solvent-based and water-based paints are suitable for decorating furniture, but it does depend on what piece of furniture is to be painted. For example, a linen cupboard which isn't used daily like, say, a kitchen cupboard, can have a less tough finish. A piece of furniture that has a lot of wear needs far more protection and therefore more coats of paint. The bare timber needs to be sanded thoroughly, then all knots must be sealed with knotting or shellac. When dry, rub down again and remove dust with a rag dipped in white spirit. Apply the primer, let it dry, sand and remove dust. It is best to apply two coats of undercoat, with each drying completely, then sand and remove any dust again. Too often this stage is neglected resulting in a pitted surface. One top coat should give a professional finish.

Some tips to remember are:

✓ Sliding parts like drawer runners must not be painted. Paint only the first inch of the sides of the drawers. Varnish the insides of drawers.

✓ Set a kitchen chair upside down on a bench to paint its legs and cross-members first. Pop a small wire nail into each foot, so that you can stand it up on the nail heads to complete the painting.

✓ Use a 15 mm (½ in) brush for mouldings, rails and legs. Take care with these details. For this part of the job it is better to thin the paint a little and using it sparingly. Apply two coats rather than risk – running and curtaining –

when too much is applied to, say, turned spindles. The instructions on each can of paint will tell you how to use a particular product. One-coat acrylic paints need to go on quickly and liberally. Solvent-based paints dry less quickly and will need more time to complete a job. Some one-coat paints don't need brushing out and laying off. Acrylic paints are non-flammable, dry more quickly but can leave brush marks. Also they suffer from being affected adversely if applied when any moisture is present in the air. It is important to check very carefully on the specification, content and details of how to apply your chosen paint.

Dragging

To totally change the look of a piece of furniture that is a plain colour and to add an interesting decorative striped pattern, you'll need a long-haired 'dragging' brush and a fairly steady hand! This technique has been used for many years on doors and surrounds. It also creates fine muted patterned stripes on furniture by keeping the brush marks vertical. A dragging brush is specially designed to give a soft, regular effect. Lay the dry brush almost flat against the wet paint and gently drag it down to make your decorative stripes. Apply a special 'paint effect' colour wash (available at DIY stores) on to a dry base colour of oil paint, working in areas about a square metre (square yard). Work

With a steady hand and a long-haired dragging brush, interesting and professional effects are possible on any surface. You get finely muted vertical stripes by gently dragging the dry brush flat against the wet second coat.

with the dry dragging brush immediately. As you go to the next area work back into the preceding striped pattern so that no apparent join is seen. This 'laying off' can be mastered very easily, and remember, as it's wet paint you can always go back over it!

Graining

I must say that I like the beauty inherent in the natural grain of wood, but sometimes we have furniture that is plain or painted. Now, however, it is possible to simulate natural grain to give a most attractive grain finish to

After applying a base coat and letting it dry, paint on a second decorative top coat to be grained with a special graining tool. Pull and rock through the wet paint to get interesting grain patterns to transform bedroom furniture in hours.

plain furniture. If the piece has an oil paint finish, just give it a key with fine wire wool, then apply a coat of the new special melamine primer (available at paint stores), followed by your choice of a base colour in matt or soft sheen. A graining 'rocker' tool kit is available at DIY stores. This easy to use tool has a 50 mm (2 in) half circular rubber end incised with a grain pattern. When pulled and rocked along the wet top coat in a straight line, amazingly you'll see what looks like open grained wood. A quicker rocking motion even produces knots in the wood. There is also a 'graining comb' in the kit which produces a straighter and closer grain effect and for a really tight grain, angle the comb at 45° so that the teeth marks of the comb on the wood are tighter together. Combine and stagger the two techniques together to add a truly convincing wood look to what was an ordinary piece of furniture.

Techniques

Victorian decorators developed extraordinary techniques to give an individual look to the porches of middle-class houses. Using only feathers, rags and sponges, and cutting their own patterns for stencilling attractive decorative features, their skill and expertise has been handed down over the years. My own grandfather was a great exponent of paint techniques. Born in the middle of the Victorian era and apprenticed at a young age, he was soon in great demand in South Wales for his painting skills. I learned a great deal from him in the mid-1940s. Much of this information has been superseded by modern techniques, like cutting stencils by machine, but skilled painters are still in demand not only for their colour sense but also for the brilliant effects that they achieve. Today, statistics show that ladies generally are better at colour coordination and painting techniques. Trompe l'œil is the ultimate in paint technique decorating. Imagine a plain, dull wall at the end of a passageway being totally transformed into a scene that actually looks real, for example, like looking out through a window on to an Italianate balcony overlooking a sunlit bay with scuttling clouds and bobbing boats – that is how good it can get!

Stippling

There are three stippling effects described here for you to get pleasure from. Transform a room that has been painted with a base colour into a professionally looking decorated room using a paint technique that is applied with a brush, sponge or rag. The great thing about this simple technique is that you can always have a second go if you're unhappy with your first attempt or if your choice of colour combination is not really to your liking once applied. After a base coat has been applied and has dried to a pleasant even colour, you're ready to apply the stipple effect. At this stage you should experiment. On a board which has been painted with the same base colour, try to get an effect that pleases you. First, apply

Crackle glazing
We are familiar with criss-cross crackle lines in old oil paintings. Achieve the same mature look on furniture by painting two coats of special crackle glazes. Worn linen chests and picture frames will be much admired after being 'mellowed' with crackle glaze.

a two-tone effect of the same colour, then try a two-colour effect. Often a two-tone scheme has a calming feeling, whereas a two-colour textured wall can be more exciting. Using a primary colour, say a deep red as a base coat, sponge your stipple effect with a pale peach colour or your own favourite combination of colours. Warm colours always give a cosy feel to a room, whereas blues and greens, the cool colours, give a more restful feeling. Get to know how colours work together in harmony or how they behave when applied as contrasting colours.

Sponge stippling is soft and gentle, whereas rag stippling is vivid and bold. Wear gloves to wet a rag in the paint, randomly stipple, and turn the rag to change patterns. A clean rag dipped in the base colour will blot out mistakes.

Before you buy your paint supply, take home some tiny pots of paint that are available at the stores, just for experimenting.

We all know the three primary colours – red, blue and yellow – and that mixed together in equal amounts you get the secondary colours. Red and yellow in equal proportions give you a bright orange, red with blue gives violet, and blue and yellow make green. Change the amounts of each and you'll change the density and tone of the resultant secondary colour. Warm colours are reds and yellows and combinations of them. Use a more intense red and you get a more vibrant feel. Cool colours, blues and greens, make us think of the country, fields and sky, a more relaxed and calmer feel. Only by experimenting can you begin to get a feel for colour and a background knowledge of how colours work for you personally. Interestingly, some artists actually use a stipple brush to get an effect usually gained by mixing colours together. For example, some French Impressionists stippled dabs of yellow against dabs of green to give the impression of a tree in full leaf. Colour experimentation is important, as is the surface on which you apply the colour. A heavily textured wallpaper will look totally different to a smoother lining paper of the same colour scheme. The textured wall will be more interesting to look at but that's not to say it is more attractive to you personally.

Brush stippling

Try out a stipple brush, available at DIY stores, on one part of the board. Pour a small amount of paint into a shallow container, and with only a little paint on the brush, delicately dab at the board to make an attractive pattern. The closer together the 'dabs', the denser the effect, but a random circular movement or an overlapping square pattern might be your choice. You have to choose which is going to be the dominant colour by a light touch or by a dense brush application. In any case, once you've experimented on your board, you'll know exactly what you are aiming for. Remember that whatever

Stippling
Stippling is something that most children learn at school. Variations are numerous – try a few. Turning a brush gives a random square effect, swirling it gives irregular curves.

you do to start, it is not there for good, so you can always use the base colour to cover mistakes such as if you concentrated too much stippling in a patch.

An alternative is to use more than one colour to stipple. Very interesting effects are possible with two or three colours applied in succession after each coat has dried. The first stippling coat can be applied sparingly and the second even more so, then the base coat is still the dominant colour of the scheme.

Sponge stippling

If you can achieve a sensitive touch with a natural sponge dipped in paint, your wall will look great with its subtle tones and shades. Stipple gently and wide apart to start; you can fill in as you go along. Add subsequent colours to create even more interesting effects.

Rag stippling

Another stippling technique is to use a wad of rag soaked in the paint. Wearing rubber gloves, squeeze the excess paint out and apply, again experimenting on a piece of stiff card or a board painted with your base colour. The more you experiment the better effect you'll get and the bolder you'll become. In fact, it becomes a joy when you're aware that you are getting effects similar to some that you've appreciated in the rooms of a country house or a municipal building. You really do see that luck and a bold approach can get some amazing results. Vary the pattern by unrolling the rag and creasing it into a tighter ball. Never use the rag without first squeezing the residual paint back into the container and never push the rag hard to the wall.

When the paint is dry, with a clean rag dipped into the base colour, get a constant pattern across the wall by obliterating the stippling just in parts where you consider the colour is too dense.

Sponge stippling

A more sensitive touch is necessary when applying the stipple effect with a sponge because slightly too much pressure will result in a solid patch. Always use a natural sponge but before starting leave it in a bowl of water to expand. Get rid of the residual water by squeezing it until almost dry. Then, with only a small amount of paint in a bowl or tray, dip the sponge just to touch the surface of the paint so as not to saturate it. Have a piece of cardboard handy for testing the desired stipple effect before application. Press the loaded sponge on to the board to remove the excess paint and check the finished effect. Immediately start your sponge stippling on the wall but go gently. It is best to spread the stipple impressions wide apart to start with; remember it is always easier to fill in rather than have to use the base colour to separate the impressions. Some rather interesting all-over effects are possible when you use two or three subsequent sponged coatings.

Rag rolling

The one big difference with this particular technique is that you should do it with a helper. The reason is that instead of getting the effect by adding paint, as in stippling, this technique involves removing wet paint. As one person rolls on paint, the second removes it by literally rolling a rag up the wall. Leave a pale base colour of a satin solvent paint to dry, then have your helper apply a diluted darker satin paint coat. Dilute by just a half but be careful to check the label for the correct solvent to use. Your rag should be about 200 mm (8 in) long when twisted into a roll of about 50 mm (2 in) diameter. The

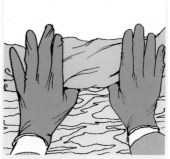

Rag rolling

Allow a base coat to dry thoroughly. Apply a second coat and immediately start rolling a rag over it. The paint is removed in part to reveal the base coat in an interesting pattern.

resulting effect is quite wonderful as you roll the rag up the wall in bands and, when dry, it will look like a piece of Chinese silk. You've now mastered the ancient painting technique of 'scumbling'.

Marbling (or feathering): once again, leave a base coat of oil-based eggshell paint to dry. An oatmeal or pale grey will give a grey-veined marble finish. Experiment with pink marble (base coat) with grey streaks, or, on a base of off-white, try a warm peach streaked on with the tip of a turkey or goose wing feather. However, for a realistic finish this effect should only be used on surfaces that could actually be marble.

The background colour is known as a glaze and can be a mix of two parts of eggshell finish, one part of scumble glaze and one part of white spirit. I always add artist colours to tint the glaze – inexpensive tubes are easily available from any art store. Pour one tablespoon of white spirit and one of scumble glaze into a non-plastic container, then add the mix to the eggshell paint. You can control the tone and depth of colour by the amount of artists' oil colour that you use. Some painters use a rag to distribute the base glaze coat and then, with the same rag dipped in white spirit, gently change the density of the colour in some areas to give interest to the background colour. You can even add a blend of a subtly matching colour, based on the look of real marble, but merge the colours so that no hard edges are seen. A very soft brush gently stroked over the merging colours will create the background ready for the veins to be added. To add the veins, dip the feather into your chosen colour, cleverly twitching it with small hand movements to create a marbled vein effect running diagonally across the background. Mix the colour washes with artists' oil paint thinned with white spirit and glaze. Check pictures of real marble and note the variation in background colour and in the veining. A natural colour base mixed with either black or white will alter tones, but your imagination will be rewarded with a surprising result if you are patient and persistent. If you prefer a heavier or thicker vein effect, use an artist's or signwriter's brush, say a No. 3. Remember that marble is a randomly patterned stone with no parallel lines but plenty of wandering vein lines. By keeping the paint workable and moistened with white spirit, you can then soften the whole effect with a wallpaper smoothing brush. Professionals use a long, flat, soft bristled brush called a 'flogger' for the final softening effect.

Once the marbling is completed to your satisfaction, there is one more task to do and that is to protect the surface. You can do this in one of two ways. One is to paint on, with a soft paintbrush, a coat of semi-gloss polyurethane varnish. Alternatively, mix a little of the base coat and white spirit with the varnish to give a more delicate look to the marbling and to make the veins appear less bold.

Stencilling

Nowadays, great strides have been made in this technique. Buy almost any design that you fancy from art shops or as kits from large DIY outlets. Alternatively, design your own or repeat a pattern already on something in

Stencilling

Cutting and using a stencil of one's own design and pattern is quite exciting because the results are immediate and simple to achieve! This circular motif was designed by my wife and used on a hall cupboard at home.

the room. If curtains have a large rose pattern, it is very easy to copy it, simplified, on to a stencil sheet or on to a thin board made non-porous with a couple of coats of lacquer. Cut out the shape with a sharp trimming knife, always working away from your fingers. Hold the stencil in position either with a 'low-tack' spray adhesive or with masking tape. Dab the brush on to the design using only a small amount of paint. Work inwards from all the edges, so as not to allow the paint to creep under the card or stencil. Apply, on to a dry base coat of universal primer, a top coat of eggshell with a brush or mini-roller, and leave to dry. The stencilling can be done with another colour of eggshell. Small sample pots of paint are available in vinyl matt emulsion if you only have a small amount of stencilling to do. If you are repeating the pattern around a room, use a spirit level to make sure that the top of the stencil or card is always horizontal. Mark each successive stencil position exactly with a pencil mark on the wall that can be matched against a registration mark on the stencil.

Liming

Time after time, on visiting some great buildings in France, I came across old furniture, doors and woodwork that had a very special, appealing look. As a young architectural student I was intrigued by the English translation which I was told was 'limed-oak', but nobody could tell me how the emphasising of the grain by making it a lighter colour than the rest of the wood was attained. Back in Wales, my grandfather once again came to my aid. It really is a simple but effective technique involving only white paint and white spirit. The technique was simply to paint on and wipe off with just enough pressure to leave the grain filled with the paint.

This adds charm and a patina of age to characterless softwoods, and is perfect for kitchen cupboards, doors and furniture. However, if you want to retain the natural grain of the wood but also to colour it, there are antique pine or light oak wood stains available. Dark blue, ebony or black base colours add drama. Modern wood stains can leave a light or dense colour and do not obscure the grain of the wood. An alternative method is to use a clear matt polyurethane varnish thinned with white spirit to seal the surface before applying the lime wash. One part white spirit to one part white paint will give a consistency that will spread evenly over the surface but when wiped off the residue will remain in the undulations of the grain. Use a dry sponge across the grain to remove the excess paint. Some specialist painters actually use an undercoat mixed with white spirit as the lime wash. You can choose eggshell, satin finish or non-drip gloss.

Coatings

Wall coatings are different from any other paint effect because, once mixed, they are of a stiffer consistency and applied to a thickness of 3 mm (⅛ in) before texturing. There are two good reasons for using a wall and ceiling coating. One is to produce an unusual textured finish and the other to successfully hide cracks and gaps in walls, concealing defects like bumps and undulations. DIY coatings come in ready-mix tubs and in bags of powder to be mixed with water. Some are available in colours but all can be decorated with emulsion paint to fit in with your decor. If you have irregularities in a wall or ceiling surface, they can easily be hidden by applying a textured finish coating. You can sculpt almost any pattern into the coating because of its stiff consistency, and it remains workable for some time (check the instructions on the pack) so you have time to perfect your chosen swirl, comb or tree bark effect.

Paul O'Grady (alias Lily Savage) was absolutely intrigued to find that it was so easy to produce a series of swirls just with a screwed up plastic bag into which I popped a pair of my socks! Wear plastic gloves to protect your hands and screw the bag into a tight ball, press it into the wet coating and twist without sliding to get a very decorative swirl. Repeat it at random, overlapping each swirl all over the wall and you'll be as thrilled with the final result as Paul was!

Textured

All textured coatings can only be applied to a wall or ceiling that has been properly prepared. This means total degreasing and then the usual stages of filling, smoothing and stabilising. After masking switches, sockets and edges, use an old emulsion brush to apply the coating to the wall or ceiling. A roller can be used but the coating will become thinner as it spreads more. Experiment with different rollers to produce different textures. I've tried elastic bands around an old hardened roller and found it gave a most interesting bark effect. Another

Textured wall coatings
Apply with a large brush, 'crossing' a couple of times to get an even finish before texturing.

experiment I tried for rolling a sand colour on to a deep green base colour was to haphazardly wind elastic bands around a long-haired lambswool roller. The startling result was a deep underwater shimmering effect. Before you begin, have all materials and tools together, working from a complete tools and materials list. Remove as much furniture from the room as possible, lay floor coverings and have a safe stepladder to hand. As

A good quality wide 'float' or scraper with a sensible handle is a boon for applying wall and ceiling coatings. It is also used for creating patterns and to smooth points on a textured surface that can occur if the consistency is too thick. Experiment on a spare board with the toothed scraper. You'll find that the recognisable comb 'shell' effect is easily achieved. Spread the coating evenly with the 'float'. Press on one point and sweep an arc!

you are going to cover only 2–3 sq m (2–3 sq yd) at a time, there is no need for a plank between two stepladders. A DIY 'hop-up' is ideal for getting to the tops of walls. Remember that the coating will cover and conceal many of the irritating blemishes that you may discover when working close to the wall. You do not have to be so fussy as you do when preparing your wall for wallpapering or painting. If you find any mould lurking from past condensation, treat it with a proprietary fungicide. Once all the areas adjacent to the walls, like architraves, window sills, switches, sockets and skirtings are masked, you should be ready to start.

Inexpensive, special rollers are available that are specially designed for patterning wall and ceiling coatings. Use one, for example, with a single diagonal groove to produce an oak tree bark effect. Another has crossing diagonal grooves to get an all over diamond pattern, but this is better in a large room. One interesting one that I found has open grooves running around it which produced a knotted bark effect. Another has concentric indents and makes a small circular interlocking pattern which looks very professional. It is easy to join each part of the pattern because the circles intertwine and are not complete circles. It looks very 'art deco'.

Swirls

The best and easiest swirls can be produced with a square stipple brush. Apply the coating liberally but don't spread it 'out', spread it 'in' instead. In other words, don't tease it out to cover more wall space, just eke it out by brushing only on the area covered by one application. You can start anywhere in the 2 sq m (2 sq yd) area and work out in any direction. The swirls are going to overlap randomly. Press the brush into the coating and immediately give one complete twist of the wrist maintaining an even pressure. The trick is not to move the brush sideways. Lift off cleanly to leave a positive swirl. This really is easy

Textured wall coatings – swirls

Wrap a sponge in a polythene bag to get a variety of patterns. A swirl is obtained by simply twisting the sponge.

and the effects are stunning. Don't leave any spaces between the swirls and you'll be amazed at how quickly a wall can be covered. Go as close to the ceiling as possible and the edge of a border is no problem because with a small brush drawn around the wall and tight to the ceiling you can professionally define the border by flattening the coating.

A sponge will also give a very satisfactory swirl effect. If you start at one side and work towards the centre you'll get a pleasing layered effect but take care to repeat each twist of the wrist with the same amount of overlap of the preceding swirl. A stipple brush lifts off very little of the coating, but a sponge, because of its nature, will need to be cleaned by dipping into a bucket of water and squeezing dry, probably after each swirl.

Combed

Once all the preparation work is completed and the first small area coated properly, run a roller over it to get a slightly thinner and more even surface. This is because a combed effect does not need to be raised too much. Use the special toothed spatula that comes with a wall coating kit. Try first to hold the comb (spatula) as if offering a dinner plate, then turn your hand upside down and apply one corner tightly to the wall so that it becomes the fulcrum or turning point. Now, gently press the comb to the wall but maintain pressure on that one corner. Sweep the comb around in a 180°

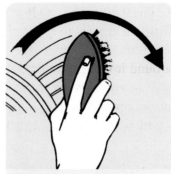

Textured wall coatings – combed

An ordinary scrubbing brush will give an interesting shell pattern.

arc to create your combed pattern. Try not to let it slip – if it does you can always start again – and keep working at it until it's second nature, then you're ready to cover the wall with wonderfully combed patterns or scrolls. Overlap only in one direction so that you get a professional looking regular pattern.

Geometric

There are rollers available that create many geometric patterns such as diamond, squares and circles. One type produces a small squared pattern with lines running alternately horizontally and vertically in adjacent squares. This basket-weave pattern can also be produced on a larger scale by cutting notches into the edge of the lid of a square plastic container. To increase your knowledge of what is available, ask at your local DIY store for brochures on rollers, spatulas and rubber serrated tools. These will give different geometric effects. For example, with a tile cement-spreader that has large teeth, you can create a herringbone pattern or a chequerboard effect, or with the rounded end of a triangular spatula, draw it vertically and horizontally at regular intervals to make a geometric harlequin design. Once the pattern has been finished, if too much coating has been raised in patches, it will harden into sharp edges. To solve this problem, hold a large plastic spatula at a low angle and draw it very lightly over the whole of the pattern.

Stipple

There are two main methods of producing a stipple effect on wall coatings. Both methods can be used to create similar effects but with slight variations.

Use a wet sponge to pat the coating to give a pitted effect. Take care not to apply too much pressure as this will bring up the coating into tiny spikes. These sharp edges play havoc with woollen garments that can snag on the tiny points (sleeves are particularly vulnerable). You'll need to rinse the sponge each time that you move to the new area. At the same time as sponging the coating, stroke the finished stippled 2 sq m (2 sq yd) area of the wall with the flat straight edge of a plastic spatula to lay down the sharp points.

Wall coatings are probably the easiest of all finishes to apply, because some licence in the application adds interest. An even coat is not essential; the stipple brush will give the whole area cohesion! Dab the brush gently; overlap each time in another direction.

Alternatively, use a stipple brush – an essential part of a wall coating kit. This rubber bristled brush is perfect for getting a regular effect over the whole of a wall or ceiling surface. Just pat the wet coating with random light strokes, moving the brush to different angles so that there is no square edge left in the coating. The resultant effect is less sharp than with a coarse sponge, but it might still be necessary to stroke down some of the pitting.

High ceilings with cosmetic cracks are sometimes difficult to maintain. Solve the problem by applying a textured coating with a long-handled roller.

A lath and plaster ceiling will probably be quite old and sagging in places. Providing it is sound, give it a new lease of life with a textured coating and a bold pattern.

You can pick a pattern to apply to a ceiling, or invent your own. Try a sponge inside a plastic bag. Just press it, scrunched up, and twist it without sliding. Overlap each stroke and you can accomplish some fascinating effects.

Painting tools

Brushes

Conventional painting brushes have for a long time been made with animal hair or bristles. Usually, these are hog (pig), ox or horse, each used for specific purposes. The best has always been hog

> **Wrap rollers, pads and brushes in cling film to keep them fresh for a long time.**

hair, the most versatile material for painting. Bristles should be tapered at the tip so that you can smooth the surface to a very fine finish ('laying off'). For painting on to timber surfaces, you'll need a range of widths, 75 mm (3 in), 50 mm (2 in), 25 mm (1 in) and 12 mm (½ in). A 'devilled sash tool' is a cutting-in brush with an angled tip, useful for painting right into corners of a sash, along the sash bars on a window frame and to get a straight line against the glass. A radiator brush has a long wire handle, so named to paint behind radiators without having to remove them. There are stencil brushes and grainers for creating wood effects (these have been superseded by the new graining tool).

Recently, paintbrushes have been developed that do not shed their bristles. These are a boon to the professional and DIYer alike. They come in all the

Painting pads

More and more DIYers are finding out how painting pads can transform their concept of painting large areas, with no fatigue or aching arms! This small kit is sufficient to do most painting jobs inside and out, oil- or water-based on wood, metal and masonry!

regular sizes and look like conventional brushes. The bristles are man-made and when you see the gleaming side of one of these new brushes you can understand why it is claimed that it will glide over the paintwork with no 'pull'.

Take time when choosing brushes, especially large ones. Wielding a 100 mm (4 in) emulsion brush for a weekend can be extremely tiring. Find the best that suits you, taking into account how much experience you've had decorating and painting. Most brushes are designed for general use on wood and metal, but wall brushes can be heavy when fully loaded. An extra wide brush might cover more area, but you must have the strength to

The paint guard is a recent painting innovation. It prevents paint creeping where it is not wanted.

wield it! Try holding a wall paintbrush by the stock (the part between the bristles and the handle). You will experience less strain in your wrist and forearm – it is the way a professional decorator has been taught to hold it. A narrow brush is easier to handle – hold it as you do a pencil. The bristles are called the 'filling' and are usually set in resin or rubber and securely held by a metal 'ferrule', tightly fixed to the wooden or plastic handle. Good quality bristles, when flexed and released, should spring back into shape. The tips of each bristle on a hog's hair brush will taper and the ends of each bristle are split into fine 'filaments', giving a soft feel to the end of the brush. Because of the density of the tip of a good brush, paint is held well and very evenly distributed.

When painting, the accepted rule is to dip the brush into the paint until the bristles are almost half covered. This will obviously vary depending on the size of the brush and the viscosity of the paint. You cannot, for example, load as much thinned paint on to a brush as you can with a more viscous paint. Use a paint kettle. They are cheap and very useful. Dispense just enough paint from the tin into your kettle for ease and comfort. Always dab the brush on the side of the container to remove excess paint. If you draw the brush across the top of the paint tin, you'll fill the rim and it will drip down the outside to obliterate important instructions. A filled rim will dry hard with the result that you'll need a hammer to force the lid on to the tin with awful results.

When you've finished using water-based paints, clean the brushes thoroughly in warm soapy water to get all the residual paint from deep within the bristles. Rinse in clean water, dry on a towel, pop on an elastic band loosely around the tip of the bristles until they are dry. This will help the bristles to retain their original shape.

For solvent-based paints, cleaning is similar but more laborious. Lay the brush on newspaper and push a small batten from the stock to the tip to squeeze out residual paint. Do both sides. Check the instructions for the type of solvent to use. Get rid of excess paint by immersing the brush in the proper solvent (usually white spirit), agitate the brush, squeeze out as much of the solvent as possible, then wash with detergent in hot water. Dry it flat on towelling before wrapping an elastic band loosely around the tip of the bristles.

There is now available an award-winning brush and roller cleaner that supersedes these old established cleaning methods. This product can totally clean a brush, even one that has been used for red paint, in less than a minute, and have it ready to use immediately in white paint! How is this done? Well, the simple answer is by centrifugal force. The brush is clasped in a holder, which is held in the chuck of your drill. By spinning for only seven seconds, inside a plastic bin, most of the paint is thrown off. Agitate the brush for five seconds in a solvent and after spinning again for seven seconds you have a dry, perfectly clean brush.

Rollers

Rollers came into their own when it was realised that enthusiastic DIYers really wanted to redecorate rooms with paint rather than wallpaper. This useful device has since developed from the simple foam or lambswool sleeve roller to more sophisticated rollers with built-in paint holders. Originally developed for painting walls and ceilings more quickly, more easily and with less fatigue, rollers come with outer coverings of foam, sheepskin or synthetic fibre. These are interchangeable on a sprung wire cage linked to a shaped, cranked handle. Rollers come in standard lengths of 225 mm (9 in) and 175 mm (7 in), but smaller rollers are available too for wood and special paint techniques. Others are shaped for corners of rooms and there is even a small two-wheel roller for pipes. Outside, use a long sleeve pile for emulsion paint, which can also be used with masonry paint on rendered walls. Gloss

Rollers

Rollers come in many types and sizes from 10 cm to 30 cm (4 in to 12 in). Roller sleeves can be made of foam, synthetic fibres or lambswool, and come in different lengths for different paints and surfaces. Use a long pile on masonry, medium pile for emulsion or oil on smooth walls and short pile for gloss on wood.

A 10 cm (4 in) mini-roller is the ideal painting tool for small areas of emulsion. It is easy to handle and even the inexperienced DIYer will get surprisingly good results.

One of the most successful inventions to benefit decorators is the 'Dandy' brush and roller cleaner that literally spins off the paint. Based on the centrifugal principle, the roller is spun in a drill and is ready for a different colour in less than a minute.

paints call for a short pile sleeve or a mini dense foam roller. Check at your DIY store, where a comprehensive guide is available, covering all types of rollers and their uses. They will also advise on a powered roller with a battery driven motor if you are contemplating painting the whole house! This gives five hours of continuous use and the paint is delivered from a portable reservoir to the roller via a long flexible hose. It is estimated that you can cover a wall measuring 4500 mm × 2400 mm (15 ft × 8 ft) in less than 10 minutes.

As with brushes, there are now available new and innovative designs of rollers. One of these has a solid central cylinder to hold the paint. A small funnel allows the paint to be fed from the tin into the cylindrical container (the roller) around which the removable sleeve is fitted. After inserting the stopper the paint is totally enclosed in the cleverly perforated core of the roller body. The simple action of rolling on the wall brings the paint to the surface of the roller to give an even coat over the whole wall without any splatter whatsoever. The great thing is that the roller can hold sufficient paint to cover an average sized ceiling or wall without having to be refilled. After you've finished, any residual paint can be poured back into the container. The kit comes with its own jug together with a clip-on base which also acts as a lid for the jug. Washing the sleeve is very simple because it literally slips off from the solid core of the roller. Rinse it under a tap with warm soapy water as you would a flannel. The kit also contains a mini-roller with a flip-over guide which allows you to paint close to a light switch, for example, without getting paint on to the sides of the cover plate. A truly innovative idea being used by professionals and DIYers alike.

Before using a roller on a wall, get a clean edge all round with a brush.

There is yet another development of a roller with an attachment that holds paint – this time in the hollow handle. Surprisingly, sufficient emulsion paint can be drawn into the cylinder by the piston type plunger to cover 6 sq m (64 sq ft) of wall surface. Without stopping you can cover 2400 mm × 2400 mm (8 ft × 8 ft) in less than two minutes. At the base of the

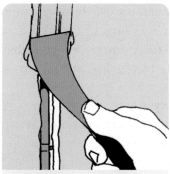

Filling knife

Cracks in plaster and in cable and pipe channels should be filled with cellulose filler applied with a flexible filling knife to ensure smooth filling.

Scraper

A scraper has the required rigidity to run behind softened wallpaper. Never use a filling knife which could hook out chunks of plaster. The scraper can also be used to scrape wood to smooth it.

cylinder is a clip to hold the filling tube firmly in the paint. The cranked roller handle keeps the roller clear of the tin of paint but is still attached to the handle. When you pull on the handle the rubber disc at the end of the piston forms a vacuum which draws the emulsion paint into the space. You do not have to wipe any parts because the whole operation is carried out easily by pushing a spigot into a tight fitting rubber ring on the clipped hose. Kits come with all parts ready assembled and with full instructions. Any paint left in the translucent cylinder handle is cleanly and efficiently returned to the paint tin by pushing the plunger. This means that there are very few parts to clean. However, every part is detachable and simply cleaned in warm soapy water.

Filling knives and scrapers

These two helpful tools are used to prepare surfaces before redecorating. They are very much the 'tool for the job in hand'. I've often been asked to advise on how to solve the problem of damaged plaster when stripping wallpaper. Invariably, the DIYer has used the filling tool and not the correct tool, the scraper. These two steel tools might look alike but must only be used for the designated purpose. A filling knife is the more flexible and could easily bend if pushed on a wall to remove wallpaper. The result is that a lump of plaster can be easily hooked out. For filling gaps and cracks in plaster walls and ceilings a high-quality steel blade held securely with rivets to a

Shave hooks

Use shave hooks to get paint off difficult mouldings. The Victorians were adept in their use because picture rails, dado rails and architraves were more intricately shaped than today. However, now we want to restore more old features in our houses, it is time to learn how to use these tools once again to solve tricky stripping problems.

hardwood handle is best.

Use a filler knife to easily smooth plaster filler into cracks and gaps in plasterwork, but first it is best to widen the inside of a crack and to remove all debris. Cover the crack with a coating of dilute PVA then force in the filler. The flexibility of the pliable blade helps to get a feather edge either side of the repair. Always wash the knife after use and wipe the metal with an oily cloth to keep it pristine. Before using it next time wipe off the surplus oil, so that it does not contaminate the next plaster repair.

Scrapers are similar in size and shape to filling knives but are thicker and have little flexibility. Used in conjunction with a wallpaper steam stripper, a good quality 75 mm (3 in) steel scraper will perform well without damaging the substrate or plaster. After removing all the wallpaper, the scraper can also be used for removing dry hard nibs and blemishes, as well as scraping off small bumps.

Paint kettles

In Victorian times, paint was often mixed by the decorator who always decanted a small amount into a separate tin or 'kettle'. This made the job easier and safer. It meant that a large tin did not have to be carried to the work site or held by hand or hook on a ladder. Nowadays, paint kettles are inexpensive, literally a fraction of the cost of a 5 litre (1 gallon) can of paint, so it makes sense to use one every time you reach for the paint and the brush. It also makes it easy to add a

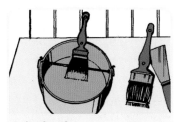

Paint kettles

Always decant paint into a paint kettle. A piece of string tied across the kettle serves as a brush rest and is useful to remove excess paint from the brush. Clean brushes with a spinning device and put an elastic band around the bristles afterwards to maintain their shape.

Painting tools

Never use a screwdriver to open a tin of paint as it will distort the lid preventing a good seal. Buy an inexpensive can opener, but use it upside down (the point upwards). Place it on the edge of the tin and gently lever.

Never use paint straight from the tin but pour 5–8 cm (2–3 in) into a plastic paint kettle, which is easy to clean.

solvent or thinners, something almost impossible with a full tin of paint. All paint kettles were previously made from galvanised metal, which made them much heavier than the present day light plastic kettles that are easy to lift, safe to handle and easily cleaned.

If the instructions from the paint you are using say stir the paint before use, always do this before decanting even the smallest amount into your kettle, then you'll be certain that all the constituents in the paint are properly mixed. This also ensures that you never ever get a build up of residue in the bottom of the tin. Return any paint that is left over to the tin and clean the kettle with the proper solvent. If, by chance, you let some paint dry hard in the kettle, it is easily removed by flexing the plastic sides.

Materials

Solvents

Solvents are liquids capable of dissolving another substance. They also act as thinners, making a particular substance, like paint, less viscous to make it flow more freely. When used in large quantities, as in a factory, precautions have to be taken under the Health and Safety Executive's Regulations, to make a safe working environment. Even in the home it is wise to ensure that you have plenty of ventilation when using solvents and thinners to dilute paints and varnishes, and it is unwise to smoke when using white spirit or any other recommended thinners for an oil-based paint. Keep all solvents and thinners in childproof containers or, better still, in a locked cupboard. It's common sense really!

Solvents are not good for the skin, even though they are sometimes used by

For a small paint job, fit a plastic bag inside a saucepan to hold the paint.

Imagine being able to paint radiators at the same time as the walls, with the same water-based paint. Radiator Clearcoat gives any standard emulsion the heat-resistant, wipe-clean properties of traditional radiator paint.

DIYers for cleaning paint from hands! I use a proprietary barrier cream when tackling a painting job that involves white spirits for oil-based paints or thinners for cellulose. Water is the solvent for emulsion paint and is used for thinning and cleaning. If you use a masonry paint on the exterior of your house, it is usually water-based. It is good practice always to thin the emulsion paints and masonry paints for the first coat. Thinning also means better penetration of the water-based paints so the substrate absorbs the coating to form a seal. Water-based acrylic paints used for a finish coat on wood give a tough sheen finish even though the solvent used is water. The vinyl, synthetic resin in emulsion paint produces a hard, washable finish, despite being water soluble in the tin.

Oil paints

Choose decorative oil paints to get an attractive, durable and hygienic finish. The base, or medium, for oil paints depends on a manufacturer's choice of the proportion of oil to resin. In the past, natural resin was chosen, but it was so slow drying that a synthetic resin was produced to supply the demand for a faster drying paint. Strong and subtle colours are available depending on the pigment used and the amount of pigment related to the amount of resin used in the manufacture of oil paint. This also makes the difference between gloss and satin. Nowadays, oil paints are available that are called 'low odour'. These paints have very little smell and no problematic fumes to irritate those DIYers with breathing problems. Doors and

Painting wood

When applying oil-based paint to wood, always paint in the direction of the grain and never put the wet brush into an area that has already been painted. 'Lay-off' from dry wood into the wet paint.

windows painted with oil-based paints should only require a wipe down with warm soapy water where dirt and dust has settled.

When repainting a surface that is sound, with no flaking or blemishes, you will only need to 'key' it with fine wire wool before applying one coat of paint. Alternatively, you can use a 'one-coat' gloss which is also formulated for use without an undercoat. Use an oil-based one-coat paint, which obliterates and glosses in one, on primed, new wood. It has a higher pigment content and is thicker in consistency, but flows easily without having to brush it out too much. A great development for professionals and DIYers.

Water-based paints

One of the most interesting developments in the manufacture of paints has been that of water-based paints like acrylics. Technological advances in the formulation of these paints mean that we now have a water-based paint that gives a tough finish on wood inside or outside the home. Advantages are that it is non-flammable, it dries quickly, has little smell and offers less risk to one's health than solvent-based products. Some manufacturers recommend using a synthetic bristle brush with their acrylic products. Another advantage is that, because one has to work more quickly, there is then less chance of leaving brush marks. One disadvantage is that you will not get a high-gloss finish on wood.

Other water-based paints are emulsions and masonry paints (ask for one with a mould inhibitor). These are covered elsewhere in this section. All water-based paints are obviously more environment-friendly than solvent-based paints, but be careful when disposing of all tins and residual paint deposits (particularly of solvents). Contact your Local Council (Environmental Department) for advice.

Coatings
Interior coatings

Interior wall coatings are very different from exterior coatings like rendering (which is a mix of sand and cement). The former are used for two main reasons: to cover blemishes and imperfections in a wall or ceiling without the need for repairing cosmetic cracks and to produce a textured surface using one of the many incised or patterned rollers, combs and spatulas designed for this purpose. The art of texturing, that is imaginatively creating a unique patterned, all-over, raised design, is covered in the section on techniques. Artex has come into our language when referring to wall coatings in the same way as Hoover did for vacuum cleaners, but coatings or textured coatings which are thicker than paint, come in various forms for different purposes. A ready-mix coating in tub form is a one-coat application requiring no undercoat. Some ready-mix coatings can fill cracks to a depth of an inch without sagging. Other coatings come in powder form for mixing with water. In these cases, follow the instructions very carefully to prevent lumps forming. Use a 'paddle' mixer fixed to your drill to get a truly professional mix – all decorators do this as they usually work with large amounts. Always sprinkle the powder on to the water and not the other way round or you will get lumps!

Coatings are best applied with an old emulsion brush, but if a light coating is wanted use a roller to spread it over a wall or ceiling. After the surface has been properly prepared and is smooth, flat and even, apply a coat of diluted PVA to act as a seal and a stabiliser. This provides a good key for the coating material so that it becomes bonded to the substrate.

Exterior coatings

Exterior coatings are usually a mix of cement, sand and lime. This mortar mix must not be stronger than the wall to which it is going to bond. For example, a higher proportion of sand to cement, about 1 to 6, is needed when applying the render to, say, a garage wall of block work or a house wall of soft bricks, whereas a mix of one part cement to four parts sand would be suitable for solid concrete or hand-fired bricks. Carry out all repairs to perished pointing, friable surfaces, old flaking paint and then stabilise the area using diluted PVA. Add either an inhibitor to the mortar or when the coating has completely dried use a proprietary surface sealer applied by either spray, brush or roller, to prevent the future problem of water penetration through an exterior render coating. Fix temporary wooden battens to contain the render within a particular area on an outside wall. It is a fallacy to believe that mortar sets or cures by drying out. The longer it is kept damp the stronger the finish coating will be. Hydration takes place as soon as water is added to the mix to create a chemical reaction for the 'curing' to begin. Types of finishes for exterior rendering are covered separately in this book.

Wallpapering

Types of covering

Wallpaper

Nobody need feel that there isn't a colour or pattern of a wallpaper to suit their taste! Machine-printed wallpapers are relatively inexpensive and produced for the mass market in a myriad of colours, designs and patterns – we've all experienced the frustration of trying to make a choice from the innumerable pattern books available in a store. The secret is to make a few notes before visiting the shop. Stick to a basic combination of colours and think in terms of large or small repeating patterns or vertical lines or even classical patterns. Think also of how much you want to spend. Last of all, do you want a vinyl, flock, grass cloth, paper-backed cotton, linen or silk (beautiful, but costly), or perhaps a coarse hessian? With your notes to hand the sales person should show you the pattern books limited to your choices.

Embossed

The use of wallpaper as a decorative wall finish was established in the UK in the sixteenth century. However, the greatest expansion of papers available and of the firms producing them happened in the nineteenth century when mechanised printing came into its own. Victorians demanded what we would call 'fussy' effects to be painted or varnished after being applied to the wall. So Anaglypta® was born. This dense paper, into which the pattern was embossed during manufacture by the use of metal dies, gave a richer effect than that of simple printed papers. The pattern remained prominent even after painting or varnishing. At this time 'flock' wallpapers, which incorporate a shallow velvet pile, producing a similar effect, were also developed. However, flock could not be over-painted when the original surface became discoloured. At the same time other wallpaper manufacturers competed by producing Lincrusta®, a rival to Anaglypta®.

Thousands of elaborate wallpaper patterns were designed to meet the Victorian demand. Some of these are still available today. However, modern day wallpaper designers have produced Victorian patterns and colours on a wide range of contemporary papers, but you will pay more for these than the standard vinyl wall coverings.

Woodchip

Wallpaper is available in a wide range, from the popular woodchip to the more exotic paper-backed fabrics. Woodchip is used a great deal by developers because it is inexpensive and it easily covers some imperfections. Small particles of chipped wood are layered between two papers giving a raised relief covering. When such a pronounced textured paper is lit by a side light, the overall look can be stronger than any blemishes, such as where two adjacent sections of a wall are not in line. Woodchip is tougher than most papers so a good sharp knife and a straight edge is best for initial cutting. Use one of the new, angled aluminium trimming guides or long sharp scissors to trim woodchip.

Linings
Lining paper

Never leave to chance that a wall covering will cover all blemishes. It is true to say that 'it is all down to preparation'! The wall has to be as flat and even as possible before hanging wallpaper. It is mistakenly believed that wallpaper will contract on drying out to cover a crack or a nib that has inadvertently been left. It is true that wallpaper will contract but only to compound the problem. The crack or the nib will show up even worse. Even heavily embossed paper needs a perfectly flat wall to get a professional finish. Lining paper will help with minor blemishes but hang it horizontally. If you are right-handed work from the right of the wall holding the concertinaed paper in your left hand and smoothing with the brush held in your right hand. (Lining paper hung in preparation for a painting technique application should be hung vertically.)

Polystyrene

One of the most common problems related to wallpapering is mould, usually caused by condensation. This is often found when a free-standing wardrobe is moved from a corner of a bedroom being prepared for decorating. Spores feed on the damp wall surface leaving a black mould. Condensation is easily explained. When you breathe warm moist air on to a cold window we all know that we get rivulets running down the pane of glass. Wherever warm moist air is in contact with a cold wall you run the risk of condensation, so this can happen inside wardrobes fixed to outside walls. Mildew on leather shoes is a good indicator of this type of condensation. One method of solving the problem is to hang sheets of expanded polystyrene on the wall before hanging the wallpaper. Clean off the mould with a fungicidal solution before stripping the old wallpaper, then compress the pieces into a dustbin liner ready for disposal. It needs to be contained, so as not to allow the contaminated paper to spread the spores. The polystyrene comes in rolls and can be hung by pasting it as you would ordinary paper. You'll find that the material is easily dented so take care handling and hanging.

Polystyrene feels warm when you lay your hand on it and this is a clue to what is happening when you hang polystyrene sheets on a wall to be covered with wallpaper. The polystyrene will retain its warmth and prevent the cold from the exterior wall travelling through to the inside wall, so condensation cannot happen. Sometimes, if the problem is bad you might need sheets up to 25 mm (1 in) thick fixed to the wall with special adhesive and faced with a laminated sheet.

Stripping

The easiest and most effective way to strip any wallpaper is by using a steam stripper. If you don't own one, it is cheap to hire one for a weekend. Follow

Put stripped wallpaper in plastic bags.

the instructions carefully and you will quickly learn how to use it. It really is amazing how swiftly one wall can be stripped with just this tool.

Scoring

In the past, paper was stripped by soaking it with a sponge after having scored it with a wire brush, a knife or a 'hedgehog' (a small spiked wheel on the end of a wooden handle). These made perforations in the paper so that the warm water could penetrate to soften the old paste. In effect what one has to do is to lessen the paste adhesion so that the paper comes away easily without leaving strands. Requiring many buckets of soapy, warm water, it proved to be a laborious operation. Meanwhile, designers and manufacturers were putting time and money into the design and development of a machine that was safe and efficient to make the job of stripping wallpaper a more enjoyable operation – the steam stripper.

Steaming

Steam strippers run off the mains so follow the instructions that come with your steam stripper and you'll have no problem using one. A floor-standing water container has a heating element to produce steam which passes through a long hose to the steam plate. The flat, tough plastic plate is not distorted by the steam so that the steam is delivered exactly where you want it and does not escape through the sides. Take all the usual precautions like protecting sockets and switches to prevent water rivulets entering the boxes to cause problems. Use coverings to protect the floor and plastic bags for disposing of the stripped paper.

Hire a steam stripper to remove wallpaper. An industrial machine is quickest.

Stripping wallpaper

Hire a steam stripper to remove the old wallpaper safely, quickly and efficiently. Make sure you read the instructions carefully. They're important for your safety and to professionally prepare a wall for repapering.

Before steam-stripping paper use a 'hedgehog' – a roller with spikes.

Once the steam is generated, hold the steam plate at your starting point. Lift the saturated paper off with a scraper whilst holding the plate at your second position. You'll make it a continuous action with no stopping – a very satisfying task, which gets immediate results.

Wallpapers that have had a coat of paint are more difficult to remove by traditional methods, but by using a steam stripper you should have no problems.

Stripping wallpaper
Always use a stripping knife to strip paper. Never use a filling knife which looks similar but is flexible. The filling knife will snag and flick out the plaster.

Certain types of vinyl wallpaper are easy to strip because they come as two layers, a top patterned plastic film and a lining paper. Sometimes you can get a sharp tool or even your fingernail behind a corner of the top layer to peel it off in one long length. You are then left with the lining paper. Some decorators leave this in place if it is still sound.

Anaglypta®

Anaglypta®, and similar embossed wallpapers, are still used today especially for authentic restoration projects. These were usually manufactured as two layers with a raised pattern. If you have to remove them, you'll probably find it a bit brittle, in which case more steam treatment will be necessary. The top layer will come off separately after steaming but you'll also have to remove the backing paper because it too will have the raised pattern on it.

Scraping

When removing wallpaper, the one problem that many people face is damage, however small, to the plaster wall. Once the paper is properly soaked, use your scraper (not a filling knife) at the correct low angle to be able to remove the paper in one long piece. Remember that your stepladder must be placed with the feet against the skirting board for your own safety. Once the first piece of wallpaper has been soaked across its width, only 520 mm (21 in), and loosened at the top with your scraper, its weight will cause it to flop down if you're working from above. However, wherever you start, check that the water caused by the steam condensing and running down the wall is not seeping behind sockets, behind the skirting board or through any protective floor covering. Use a sponge to continually mop up the rivulets. Scrapers come in various widths and, as with all steel tools, you get what you pay for. Buy the best you can afford. A 100 mm (4 in) wide scraper is ideal for wallpaper stripping. Get one that has a long wooden handle riveted to the steel, which should be in one piece through to the tip of the handle. A longer handle allows you to get lower angles preventing it from digging into the plaster.

Disposal

Stripping wallpaper can be a messy job but need not give problems if you are properly organised. We all know that getting rid of the floppy, wet lumps of paper and picking bits off the floor and from our footwear is the irritating part of the preparation! Solving these problems is simple. Start by using plenty of floor covering and have two large plastic sacks open near you. A professional decorator always rolls down the bag to halfway so that the tight roll provides a firm edge that is not going to collapse and the folded pieces of wet paper can go straight into the bag. You'll never again carry around bits stuck to your shoes. Always first fold the pieces paste side in and then fold it as many times as you can before it goes into the bag. Screwed up paper takes up much more room, and of course your hands could get covered with paste.

Hanging
Measuring

Wallpaper rolls are not necessarily of a standard width and length, however most machine-printed wallpapers in the mid-price range are 10 m (33 ft) long and 520 mm (21 in) wide. When you contemplate a DIY wallpapering job calculate how many rolls you'll

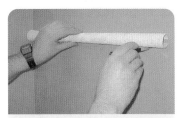

For the first 'drop' (the piece to be hung) at a corner, mark 12 mm (½ in) in for the plumb-bob line. Mark the position, holding a roll into the corner.

Hanging wallpaper:

1. Cutting guide in position.
2. Hang the 'drop' as usual with about 10 cm (4 in) of overhang for trimming; slip the cutting guide under the paper, tight to the wall.
3. Brush the wet paper tight to the guide and cut along the front edge.
4. Remove the guide and brush the paper down to a perfect line with the skirting.

Position a stepladder safely, feet against skirting board.

comfortably need for a particular room. Once you have made the calculation, write that number on top of the room door and it's there for good!

First measure the length, width and height of the room. For a standard roll, divide the roll length by the height figure, say 2.4 m (8 ft), giving approximately four strips (or 'drops') from each roll. There are other considerations but we'll get to them later. Add two room lengths and two room widths together to get the measurement right round the room. For example, a room of length 4.2 m (14 ft) and width 3 m (10 ft) gives 14.4 m (48 ft). The number of rolls needed to paper this room, 12, is found by dividing the total distance round the room by the number of pieces from one roll (48 ÷ 4). The doors and windows have been included to allow for wastage. Now, if the paper has a large repeating pattern, you'll have to line up the pattern when hanging it thereby having a certain amount of wastage at the top of each drop. Check by how much when you're looking through the pattern book and take into account the following – 12 rolls will cover the walls without a drop repeat. So, 12 rolls at four pieces to a roll makes 48 pieces to hang. If a repeat pattern wastes, say, 300 mm (12 in) at the top of each piece, you'll need another 48 × 300 mm, which is 14.4 m (48 ft) – an extra two rolls. In this case, you'll have to order 14 rolls for the drop-patterned paper whereas for a non-repeating pattern paper you'll need only 12 rolls.

Cutting

The old way of trimming wallpaper was to crease the paper before cutting it with scissors. However, at the ceiling and at the skirting this calls for a certain amount of skill when following the crease line, so with the pasted paper tucked into the ceiling angle and with about 100 mm (4 in) spare, either use the Arris wallpaper trimmer or the Harris cutting guide as featured on page 51. Use a hanging brush to force the paper back into place. Always work at the ceiling first, then do the same at the skirting angle. Slide up each subsequent piece of paper to butt against the last one. Repeat the action of creasing and trimming. Do the same around architraves, window frames and electrical fittings.

The Arris powered wallpaper trimmer is foolproof and will give professional straight cuts. The long guide that fits into the joint, at say a skirting board or an architrave, ensures that the cut is true.

Only stand stepladders parallel to a wall when using two to support a plank.

Manufacturers are continually striving to make the DIYer's life easier and their products more economical, and to help us get a professional finish. Nowadays, scissors and wallpaper knives are no longer necessary because the Arris' award-winning proprietary electric cutter is available which cuts the paper directly on the wall. There is no need to even lift the pasted paper. This ingenious tool is foolproof and there are absolutely no problems at ceiling angles or at corners. Cutting around a door frame is simplicity itself. It even cuts through overlaps to give a perfect butt join. Electrical fittings do not have to be unscrewed because the blade point cuts tight to the cover plate. This precision cutter is battery powered and cuts standard, heavy duty and textile wall coverings. As a bonus it can also be used for cutting cloth patterns for tailoring. You have full control by means of a simple pressure switch. Insert the blade-point, like very tiny scissors, at an angle underneath the wallpaper, ease the runner into the crease which then positions the machine for cutting by pulling the tool backwards. This tool is indispensable for perfect wallpapering.

Pasting

The days of flour and water paste have long gone but the technique of pasting paper is the same as the Victorians practised. Nowadays, pastes are manufactured for special purposes, so

After papering rooms, write the number of rolls used on top of each door, for next time!

choose exactly the paste that is recommended for your particular wallpaper. When you begin to unroll wallpaper, tucked inside will be a specification and instruction leaflet. These instructions are the result of much research and must be followed to get perfect results. The type of paste, the soaking time for each piece of paper and the method of hanging are all important. For example, if you soak one piece of paper for two minutes and the very next one inadvertently for four minutes, the second piece will stretch and become longer than the first, so patterns aren't going to match and the subsequent contraction of each as they dry out will be different.

Different pastes are available for different papers: standard paste for lightweight papers; heavy duty paste for embossed and heavier wallpapers; ready-mixed paste formulated for paper-backed fabrics; and border paste

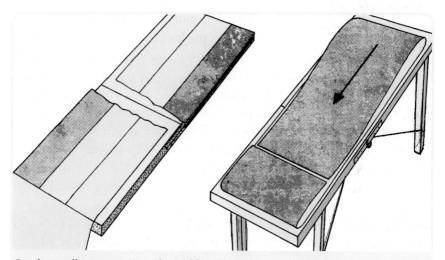

Pasting wallpaper on a pasting table

Make sure the wallpaper overlaps the edge of the table to prevent the paste getting onto the face of the paper. Slide the paper to each edge in turn.

After applying the paste, fold the paper as shown and allow it to soak for the recommended time. Lay the long end of the paper to the top of the wall.

in tubes for solving the problem of open joints and borders which are notoriously difficult when sticking on to vinyl wallpaper. Spores and mould are more commonly found under vinyl wallpapers, so check on the instruction leaflet and get a special paste that has a fungicidal additive.

In some situations, like around radiators, you can paste the wall and not the paper.

Paste standard wallpapers evenly down the centre, brushing out in turn to each edge that overlaps the pasting table. Fold over one end and leave to soak for the recommended time.

Cut the first piece of paper about 150 mm (6 in) longer than you need. On the back of the paper, with a pencil, write a capital T for the top and the number 1, indicating the hanging sequence. When you begin pasting, put part of the roll on a clean covering on the floor. Brush a long strip of paste about 200 mm (8 in) wide along the centre of the paper. Slide the paper to the far edge of your pasting table to overlap about 3 mm (⅛ in) and then paste the far strip. The overhang prevents paste seeping under the edge of the paper on to its face. Slide the paper towards you, making the front edge overhang the pasting table and paste this nearest strip. Work out from the centre in a herringbone fashion ensuring that there is an even covering of paste. Work fairly quickly so that the whole length of the paper is covered in seconds and the soaking time of the first and last pastings are as similar as possible. After pasting about 1500 mm (5 ft) make one fold in the paper, paste to paste, lining up the edges. Slide the

If you choose cotton-backed vinyl wallpaper, paste the wall not the paper.

rest of the paper on to the board and repeat the process. Fold longer pieces of paper into a concertina, always paste to paste.

Thin papers can go straight on to the wall without soaking, but standard and thicker papers must be soaked for exactly the recommended time.

DIY beginners can use a roller and paste to get an even covering on wallpaper.

However, the recommendation for certain wallpapers might be to paste the wall rather than the paper. These wallpapers are usually hand-printed or of a more delicate type. Paste a vertical band about 600 mm (2 ft) wide, which means that for the next piece, the problem of pasting on to the face of the paper is overcome. If you find a large pasting brush tiring, try using a short pile roller.

Ready-pasted wallpaper, usually vinyl, is also available. The paste is wetted by immersing each roll separately in a trough of water on the floor under the hanging position. Again, it's important to soak for exactly the prescribed time. Lift the top end slowly, bring it up to its hanging position, letting the residual water run back into the plastic trough. Follow the instructions for unrolling and hanging. For example, they might suggest you use a sponge for smoothing the wet paper.

Hanging

Only hang wallpaper when the ceiling has been redecorated and the woodwork painted – you can allow paint to creep on to the walls when covering architraves and skirting boards. This really is good practice because it ensures that if the paint line is not absolutely straight, the paper will give a straight edge along the whole length. If you are hanging a very bold patterned paper, start at the centre of a chimney breast and work your way around the room to the door frame. Then work your way around the room from the other side of the chimney breast to stop at the door. If there are two windows on one wall opposite the door, mark a centre line between them and start hanging from there, working out either side.

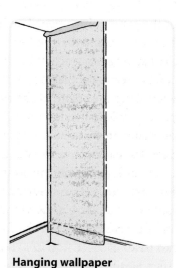

Hanging wallpaper
Start the papering in a corner with the paper overlapping the adjacent wall by about 12 mm (½ in).

First you need to mark a vertical line on the wall, against which your first piece of paper (the drop) will be positioned. This is because the walls and corners of a room are usually out of square. The best way to obtain a vertical line is the struck chalk mark. Don't use a pen or pencil, it's possible that the marks can creep through to the surface of the paper. Chalk the string of a plumb bob, pin it at the top, hold your foot against the weight

Hanging wallpaper:

(1) cutting guide in position;
(2) hang the 'drop' as usual with about 10 cm (4 in) of overhang for trimming; slip the cutting guide under the paper, tight to the wall; (3) brush the wet paper tight to the guide and cut along the front edge;
(4) remove the guide and brush the paper down to a perfect line with the skirting.

at the bottom and strike the chalk string against the wall. The position of the plumb (vertical) line will govern the position of the first piece of paper. If it's in a corner of the room, mark its position by holding a roll of paper against the corner but deduct 10 mm (⅜ in) from its length. The reason for this is that the 10 mm of the first piece to be hung will be actually pasted on to the adjacent wall and the other edge of the piece will be tight to the plumb line. When working on the adjacent wall the first piece of the second run will be plumbed from another line but just to cover that 10 mm of paper, ensuring complete cover of a corner joint.

Then, unfold the top half of the pasted paper and slide it against the plumb line. Allow a couple of inches at the top for trimming. Using a hanging brush, gently smooth down the centre of the paper and out to the edges so that no air bubbles are left. Don't press too hard otherwise you'll get paste oozing out at the sides. Gently unfold the bottom half and repeat the action, again using the hanging brush to press the paper against the skirting board. Each subsequent piece of paper will be slid to butt against the last one. Wipe surplus paste off skirting boards as you proceed – never let it harden, you'll forget it's

It's not a good idea to paper over existing wallpaper – you'll get bubbles.

there until it dries dull. A seam-roller is useful to flatten down the edges of each butted piece of paper at the seams, but don't use it on embossed paper. If any surplus paste appears anywhere on the surface of the wallpaper, wipe it off quickly, but gently, with a clean, damp sponge using a lifting, not rubbing, motion.

Chimney breasts

The external corners of chimney breasts are rarely truly vertical, so wallpaper will not look vertical after it has turned the corner. Also, if about half the width of the roll has to be pasted to the side of the chimney breast, often it ends up in folds. The trick to solve the problem is to cut the length of paper so that it only overlaps 12 mm (½ in) on to the side wall after having pasted it to the front. Then

Start hanging paper with a large pattern central to a fireplace or focal point.

use the next piece of paper to cover the overlap by 10 mm (⅜ in). Scissors are rarely successful for cutting lengths of paper so use a sharp trimming knife and a steel straight edge. However, a proprietary electric cutter makes a perfect butt joint where the two pieces overlap.

When wallpapering on a chimney breast, crease and cut the paper along the mantle shelf first. The paper will fall down either side after cutting diagonals each end. Then trim and brush the paper under the shelf as far as the upright of the surround. Take the weight of the pasted paper, otherwise it will tear. Never ever tug at wet wallpaper. Little nicks in the paper will help you turn it around small mouldings.

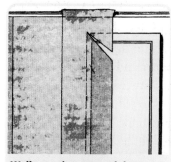

Wallpapering around doors

Papering around a door frame is not difficult if you follow these instructions but be ready to wipe off a lot of residual paste from the frame! Butt the piece of paper that hangs against the architrave to the last piece and allow it to overlap the door. Cut off the surplus paper and cut a diagonal into the paper following the mitre of the frame. Use a proprietary cutter to get perfectly straight cuts at the side and top of the frame or crease the paper and cut it carefully with a pair of scissors (or a trimming knife and straight edge).

Doorways

When wallpapering around a doorway, be prepared to wipe off paste from the door frame as you go! Using the frame as a guide, cut a diagonal up into the mitred corner of the architrave and crease the paper into the upright at the side and into the horizontal above the door. Trim the paper as already described. Electric cutters give a straight, clean cut the whole height of an architrave making it look very professional. Repeat on the other side of the door frame to leave a small gap above the door which is easily filled with a cut-to-size piece of paper. One important point to remember, if you're using a patterned paper, the pattern on all three pieces must be matched.

Electrics

Depending on the age of your house you'll have either round switches or

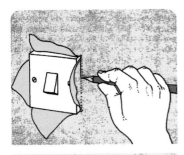

Wallpapering around light switches

Older round switches will not unscrew so trim the wallpaper close to the switch base.

You can unscrew and remove square switches and sockets (after turning off the power at the mains switch box!). Trim the paper so that 3 mm (1/8 in) goes under the switch cover.

square ones. The round ones are usually fixed. The square ones you can unscrew and lift off. You'll obviously get a much neater job if you can tuck the cut ends of the paper underneath the switch so you must turn off the electricity on that circuit. Turn on the light and switch off the circuit at the consumer unit. Either tape the switch in that position or, if it's a removable fuse, take it out and put it in your pocket. Turn off the light switch and lift the switch plate a little by undoing the screws. You will have to make straight cuts around the switch plate so that at least 12 mm (½ in) of paper tucks underneath the switch plate before screwing it back into position. Hang the paper down over the switch and cut out from the centre to the corners or edges before trimming and brushing the paper back into place. The same applies to a socket outlet but make certain that the circuit is switched off by plugging a light into the socket. Then repeat the process at the consumer unit as described above.

Window openings

The easiest method to paper around windows is to paper the 'reveals' and the 'soffit' first. These are the recessed parts of the wall nearest and adjacent to the window frame. Paper these, overlapping the main wall by about 12 mm (½ in). Continue to paper the main walls covering that small overlap. The alternative, and more professional way, is to paper the wall and reveals in one, in which case start above the window at the centre. Paper right into the window frame from the ceiling and continue either side until you come to the top corners of the window frame. When you hang ceiling-to-floor lengths either side of the window, cut the paper at the top of the opening and at the window sill with straight cuts so that you'll have a hinge. You then brush it on to the reveal. Crease and cut against the

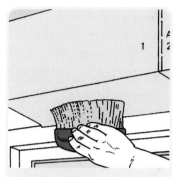

Wallpapering around windows

When papering around a window opening, always paper the 'reveals' and the 'soffit' first. These are the recessed parts of the wall nearest and adjacent to the window frame. Start at the centre above the window and continue to the frame.

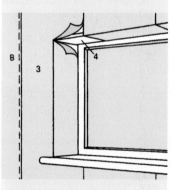

Wallpapering around windows

Cut and fold the ceiling-to-floor lengths of wallpaper either side of the window. Cut at the top of the opening and at the window sill so that you have a sort of hinge. Tightly brush this to the frame and trim. The short pieces under the window are the easiest!

window frame in the usual way. The short bits that are left to be hung underneath the window sill should come as light relief – they will be easier and quicker!

Some tips

1   After a wall has been stripped, filled, levelled and sanded it is good practice to 'size' (seal) the entire wall. Propriety sizes are available but diluted PVA is better although, perhaps, a little more expensive. Some decorators size with a diluted mixture of the same paste used for the particular wallpaper. Obviously the compatibility factor will make the adhesion even stronger.

2   A conventional radiator need not be removed from the wall to paper behind it. Transfer the positions of the bracket to a piece of wallpaper and make two slits from the bottom to the top mark of each bracket. Allow 100 mm (4 in) extra on the length of wallpaper at the skirting board position. Gently drop the pasted paper so that the slits coincide with the positions of the brackets. A long handled roller is best to roll it to the wall. Finish by carefully trimming at the skirting board.

3   Never attempt to paper a stairwell on your own. Hang the longest drop first. Your helper will need to take the paper's weight whilst you start hanging at the ceiling. To work at height, use a scaffolding board supported by a stepladder on the landing and a ladder against the head wall. Position the

scaffolding board so that you can reach the ceiling comfortably. In your calculations, allow for extra paper where it meets the angled stringer at the side of the stairs.

4 Flock paper is attractive to many people but it can prove difficult to hang. Instructions for pasting come with each roll, but sometimes you'll find that the edges are not perfectly straight. To get a professional finish to the butted joints, make an overlap and then cut through both thicknesses and remove both spare strips. Gently press back the edges and you'll get a perfect joint. Again an electric cutter will make a clean, neat joint. Never use a hard seam roller, it will mark the flock. When using the hanging brush, it's also a good idea to protect the flock with a piece of standard wallpaper.

5 It's easier when two people are working together to wallpaper a ceiling. Even though the pieces of paper are longer, the concertinaed strip end can be held by your assistant whilst you hang the remainder from the starting point. Methods and techniques are basically similar to papering a wall. Erect a platform of scaffolding boards from which to work and work backwards from your starting point, positioning the first piece against a side wall. Remember the rules for working around electric fittings. Switch off, check for power, remove shades, make star slits in the correct position to feed through the bulb holder and cable, then trim around the rose as for a light switch.

To clean marks off wallpaper, try the backs of crusts of white bread!

Tiling

Tiling changed from being strictly a professional's job to a DIY enthusiast's project with the introduction of new technology in tile manufacture, tiling tools and adhesives. It is now possible for anyone to create a beautiful, tough and hygienic wall finish. A new range of Plasplugs tiling tools helps to make any tiling job easy, speedy and enjoyable. Tile adhesive and grout are now combined in one tub for easy application. They give a smooth finish to the joints between tiles and contain anti-mould ingredients.

Mosaic tiles come already stuck to a backing sheet. They are ideal for curved walls. After grouting in the usual way, leave the residual grout powder to dry – you can use it as a polish.

Removing tiles

Because of the lasting qualities of Victorian and Edwardian tiles, still admired in many homes, we might still be confronted with problems when we are planning to renovate. Quarry floor tiles, for example, were a favourite floor covering for kitchens, passageways and downstairs WCs. These tiles are never laid on a suspended wooden floor but always on a concrete solid floor and so are sometimes very difficult to remove. The fired clay tiles were manufactured mainly in Staffordshire but the famous brand of Heather Brown quarry tiles came from Ruabon in North Wales. The distinctive blue, red and buff colours of these unglazed tiles with their silky surface finish are still being produced today.

Cork tiles are warm – and attractive on walls too.

You must loosen the adhesion of the screed into which the quarry tiles were buried to remove them. You might find a loose or rocking tile, in which case simply put your bolster chisel at a low angle underneath an adjacent tile and strike with a club hammer. Otherwise

Vinyl floor tiles, properly glued with tight joints, provide a waterproof surface.

a series of holes drilled along the edge of a tile with a masonry bit will give gap for the bolster chisel. Once you've removed all the tiles, clean off the residual nibs to leave a flat clean surface. Any undulations can be filled with a 'self-levelling' cement available at DIY stores.

If you have a large area of floor or wall tiles to remove, a compressor with a small spade chisel (similar to a Kango) will do the job in no time and with less energy expended! Some of these work with a hammer-like action that you can easily control. You can ease the chisel under the edge of the first tile and proceed with ease along a whole row of tiles. Obviously this would be too heavy for thin ceramic wall tiles, say on a stud partition plasterboard wall in a bathroom.

You can't save tiles that have been cemented in place for years. To remove them from a brick wall, tap or drill each to make a crack. It makes it easier to lever them off in pieces.

Removing ceramic tiles is much easier than taking off quarry tiles. They are usually bedded in a plaster-like tile cement and once the first tile has been broken up and removed, the rest should come off easily by prising with a bolster chisel or similar. Because a broken tile edge can be sharp, obviously take precautions – wear gloves and safety goggles. Use floor coverings and have a bucket to hand for dropping broken tiles into immediately they are removed. Remember that slithers of tile can damage a floor when inadvertently walked on. When working around fittings like taps and showers, take extra care.

There is always a tedious second stage to removing wall tiles. Small patches of tile cement will invariably be left and these

It's always easier to carry out a job with tools specifically designed for a particular task. This long-handled tile remover is one such tool. You get incredible leverage and the steel blade slips under tiles with ease. The sharp blade also deals with residual cement.

will need cleaning off. A power tool with a disc can be used but, of course, it produces dust, so you'll have to protect yourself with tight fitting goggles and a mask that has a special filter for fine dust. If you consider the dust is too much of a problem in that particular room, there's no alternative but to chisel or scrape. In order to get a professional flat finish to the new tiling job, it is essential that the wall is flat and clean before sealing the plaster with a coating of diluted PVA to make a sound base.

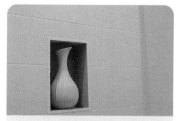

Don't be afraid to be ambitious with tiles. Plastic edge strips give a clean crisp edge to corners, sills and open shelf spaces. Tiles provide a hygienic and decorative surface, but they don't have to be dull!

It is prudent to check levels once the tiles have been removed from the wall or floor in readiness for new ones and before you seal the surface. If you suspect that the wall is not properly vertical or that the floor slopes, now is the time to check with a long batten straight edge and spirit level. Remove any bumps and fill hollows with a one-coat plaster. If two walls are adjacent at the lowest part of the sloping floor, take off the skirting boards, and if a door opening is involved, you might have to shorten the door by planing the bottom. Be sure to take into account the threshold and the adjacent floor. With all this in mind, use a self-levelling compound or mix sand and cement in the proportions of 1 to 4 to level the floor. Brush on a PVA seal before the mortar. Use a long batten with your spirit level laid on top to ensure that the repair is level ready to take your new tiling.

Use a builder's square to get a perfect right angle when laying floor tiles.

Battens

A simple aid to help plot the exact position of the tiles on a wall is a DIY batten gauge-stick. Lay a piece of straight batten with a 25 mm × 12 mm (1 in × ½ in) cross-section on the floor and lay tiles along it in a straight line. Leave the appropriate spaces for grout. Mark carefully on the batten the position of each tile and space or joint. If the tiles you

Tiling – setting out

To help set out the walls correctly for tiling, use three battens: one marked out as a gauge-stick and the other two nailed to the wall at right angles to each other to support the tiles. The gauge-stick must be marked accurately by laying tiles and spacers on the floor against the stick. Mark the centre of a plain wall for the first tiles. Arrange the tiles centrally to a window.

Undercut by chopping out

You will have to relay quarry tiles if they have been laid on a bad screed (too much sand). Use a 24 oz hammer and a bolster chisel to left them. Chip off surplus cement after soaking them in a cement cleaner – follow the manufacturer's instructions. Lay a new screed with a damp-proof membrane beneath.

are using have spacing lugs, the spaces will be uniform and pre-set, otherwise use plastic spacers to give the correct positioning. Make a second batten gauge-stick if your tiles are not square. The gauge-stick can now be held against the wall, but use a spirit level to ensure verticals and horizontals are correct and the exact position of tiles is marked on the wall.

To help set out a wall correctly for tiling, two battens can be nailed in temporary positions predetermined by the starting point. For example, if you are going to be tiling around a window in a bathroom, full tiles should start underneath the window. Check with your gauge-stick how many tiles are needed from the window sill to the skirting board or to the floor. If, say, it is three and a half, your first nailed horizontal supporting batten must be fixed underneath the third tile down. Start laying on this batten, working upwards so that the whole section is supported on the batten until the cement has gone off. The same applies with a vertical batten against a side wall. You can actually mark the position of the tiles accurately on these supporting battens by laying your gauge-stick alongside. With the use of your spirit level the battens should be fixed at right angles to each other ensuring a perfect finish.

Special dado tiles are available if you're tiling only halfway up a wall. These tiles are matched to your full tiles and give a very professional finish to the job. They come in plain, rope design, classical

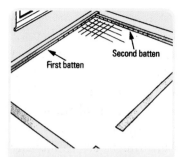

A common method of laying floor tiles is the 'square'. Fix temporary battens at exactly 90° (use your builder's square) to give you a starting point opposite the door. Use a spirit level to get the tiles flat. Work back to the door, checking constantly with your 'square'.

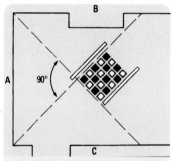

Another common pattern for laying floor tiles is the 'diagonal' or 'diamond' pattern. Transfer the length of the shortest wall (A) to the adjacent walls (B and C) to get a square. Draw diagonals as shown in the drawing and use your builder's square to check for a right angle. Use two temporary battens to guide the tiles as you lay them. Hire a special tile cutter with a diamond wheel to cut the tiles near the walls.

Plot positions of tiles on a wall with a 1 m (3 ft) gauge-stick, with marks of tiles marked on it.

designs and other patterns. If you are tiling a bathroom to a halfway mark, don't be tempted to work from the floor. It is better to have full tiles around the edge of the bath, then work up from a temporary batten fixed to support the lowest row of full tiles.

Cementing

Once you've planned where to start tiling a room, on which wall and against which focal point, fix your supporting battens in preparation for spreading the tile adhesive. Lift out the adhesive from the tub using a separate scraper tool (a very useful tool for carrying adhesive to the wall) not a serrated spreader (this is for levelling the tile cement) which could get the adhesive over the handle. Often tile adhesives come with a special spreader with teeth of a particular size suitable for that adhesive. Using the scraper tool, spread the adhesive over an area of about a square metre (square yard) and use the toothed spreader to form ridges by dragging it horizontally through the adhesive. Wipe any excess adhesive from the spreader with your scraper tool and put it back into the tub. Never allow the scraper to dry without cleaning it first. Dry it with a towel and apply a thin film of oil to protect the steel. Lay the first tile at the corner angle made by the guide batten. Suction is improved by making horizontal ridges with the spreader such that the tiles are less likely to slip.

Tile in small areas at a time. Apply the cement with a filling knife, then use a serrated spreader to form undulations which are essential for the adhesion process.

With your level guide batten temporarily in place, start spreading the tile cement. Lift it with a separate tool so that the back of the serrated spreader is kept clean. Keep the cement lines even and horizontal. As you tile, twist each one to get good adhesion.

Matching border tiles can add to the overall attraction of a well-tiled bathroom, but make sure that the tiles are designed to match your chosen pattern. Border tiles are applied in the same way, but they must be properly spaced and level!

There are many types of tile cement on the market for the DIYer. Some come as powder to be mixed with water. These will have explicit instructions which must be followed. It is essential that the powdered tile adhesive is sprinkled on to water and not the other way round as this will produce lumps. Ready-mixed adhesives come in tubs and have a circular protective plastic covering to prevent drying out. If there is adhesive left in the tub after finishing a job, scrape it from the sides and level it out, then

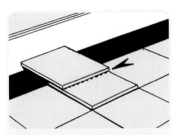

Floor tiling – cutting edge tiles

Place a tile on top of the last full tile. Use a low-tack pad to hold it in place. Place another tile on top of it touching the wall or edge. Score along the first tile. When cut, the part showing will fit the gap exactly.

push the protective plastic cover on to the tub top so that it will not lose any moisture content and be dried out the next time you want to use it. Make sure that the lid is securely fixed. There are tile adhesives available with additives which prevent against mould and against water penetration (they are waterproof). Some types are heat proof, others are blended to be used as tile cement and as a grout. If the tiled area is to be subjected to water, for example, in a shower cubicle, use waterproof tile cement. Anywhere else a standard tile adhesive is suitable.

Mark lines at right angles and work on one quarter of the floor at a time. Lay the first tile carefully against the crossed lines, twisting it slightly to get good contact.

Without letting it slip, very gently lift the tile with a trowel to check that it is completely covered with adhesive.

Having laid tiles with an attractive border almost to the wall, measure carefully the distance required for a cut tile (allowing for grout lines). The cut edge goes against the wall!

Positioning

The easiest wall to tile is a plain flat one with no door or windows. Always plan to finish with full tiles at the top of the wall. Use a gauge-stick to mark the positions of the tiles from the ceiling to the skirting, where a cut tile will probably be needed. Nail a temporary long batten to support the lowest row of whole tiles. Use a spirit level before the final fixing. Find the centre of the wall and, with the aid of a gauge-stick, mark the positions of tiles and spacings as far as the corner. Setting out tiles is very easy if you work carefully. If you've positioned your centre line correctly you'll have equal cut tiles either side of the room. When tiling around a window, as well as centring the tiles, plan to position a row of full tiles below the window sill as described previously. Your gauge-stick is an invaluable tool in the preparation, arrangement and positioning of the starting point. The top of a handbasin is generally about 250 mm (10 in) above that of the bath. You might be tempted to start your tiling with whole tiles above the basin but then you'll probably find that you'll have a row of cut tiles along the top of the bath – not a good idea! Start with full tiles along the top of the bath so that you'll only have a short row of cut tiles over the top of the handbasin.

There is no set pattern to laying out floor tiles. One way is to set out tiles from the centre of the room so that you have an even border all round the edge. To find the centre, with a helper, stretch a chalked string from the halfway point on two pairs of opposite walls. Having marked the halfway

Fix a temporary batten as a starting point for laying the first row of tiles. The batten can be removed after the tile adhesive, supporting rows of tiles, has hardened. Apply the tile adhesive from the tub with a scraper, not the spreader. Then use the spreader to obtain a uniform layer of the combed ribbing, ready for laying the tiles. Work on an area of about a square metre (square yard) at a time. As you lay a tile, twist it a little to ensure that it's firmly bedded. Place plastic spacers between the tiles to get an even grout line. Use a  proprietary grouting tool to apply and work in the grout. A wooden handled 'squeegee' type is best with a neoprene blade (it is gentle on the tiles and gets the grout into the joints). Grout residue on the tiles acts as a wonderful polish!

point on the walls ensure that the string crosses at right angles then fix each of the four ends to the floor near the skirting board. Carefully pluck the string to leave strong chalked positioning marks on the floor. Always 'dry' lay tiles in one area from the centre to the wall to check what space is left at the skirting. If one particular wall is more exposed and more in your eye line, it's easy to adjust the centre position as you wish.

Grouting

Floor tiles should be left for at least 12 hours before grouting. Nobody must walk on them during this time because the slightest movement of one tile will affect the bonding process. Some spacers can be left in to be grouted over, but if you've used DIY spacers you can remove them after about 24 hours. Manufacturers recommend a wait of anything between 36 and 48 hours before cleaning off the floor ready for grouting. Many tile manufacturers advise which grout to use whether it's a premix, which

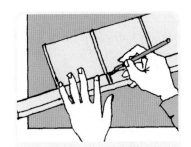

Wall tiling – gauge stick

Lay the tiles on the floor at the correct spacing. Mark a straight edge to coincide with the tile size and the grout joint.

comes in a tub, or a powder grout which has to be mixed with water to a creamy consistency. Add the powder to the water and mix only enough to

Floor grout is mixed to specific proportions and viscosity. A special spreader helps it to flow into the joints to completely fill them, but it must not be too sloppy or it will not set. Once it begins to cure, use a damp sponge to create a smooth surface.

Wear gloves when grouting the joints. Knee pads prevent future 'ache' problems and a grouting tool with a neoprene blade makes the job quick and easy!

Manufacturers produce excellent tubs of water-resistant cement that also acts as a grout. Use a grout spreader to cover a square metre (square yard) at a time, working the grout deep into the joints. Use a little at a time to prevent bubbles in the joints.

last for about half an hour because after that time it could become unworkable. Cover only a small area at a time and work the grout into the joints with a sponge or a wooden batten that fits comfortably between the tiles. If you use a sponge, make it a close textured man-made one rather than an open textured natural sponge. Have a bucket of water to hand so that you can keep the sponge clean but squeeze it almost dry before spreading the grout. The grout should be lifted from the container with a straight-edged spatula, but the manufacturer's instructions might ask you to pour it on to a small area so that it flows into the grout joints. Leave the grout to harden in the joints for the recommended time before gently wiping off the surplus with a damp sponge. Rinse frequently with clean water until only a thin film is left over the tiles. This film will dry as powder which can be polished off with a dry cloth. To avoid any chance of softening the grout, avoid washing the floor for at least a week.

Use waterproof grout for showers and baths, but epoxy-based grout for worktops.

Grouting a ceramic-tiled wall is a pleasurable DIY job because it is easy and satisfying. A white grout on coloured tiles or coloured grout used cleverly can lift a tiled wall to a new dimension. Amazingly a tiled wall, before it is grouted, can look disjointed. Minor variations in the positioning of tiles can easily lead one to believe that one has not been too careful. However, once the grout has been applied, hardened and the tiles polished, the result is always surprising! Instructions come on every pack or tub of grout and they are there to be followed. Do it and you'll be assured of a professional finish.

Replacing

Ceramic wall tiling is chosen not only for its aesthetic qualities but because it is hard wearing, hygienic and made to last a long time. However, you might at some time discover a cracked tile that needs replacing. This can happen either by accident or by movement in the fabric of the building. I always recommend that when ordering tiles, order more than you immediately need not only to cover any wastage such as accidentally breaking tiles when scoring, but also for emergency purposes like replacement. To replace a damaged ceramic wall tile, you'll first need to remove as much grout as possible from around it. There are grout remover tools available but be certain to get one

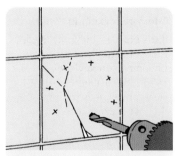

Replacing a cracked tile

The only way to successfully remove a damaged tile is to loosen it in parts, sufficiently enough for small sections to be taken out. So that surrounding tiles are not chipped, remove the centre of the damage tile first by drilling a number of marked holes.

that is slightly narrower than the grout space. These are short-handled tools with a hardened metal, fine-toothed scraping end. Take great care to keep the tool in line with the edge of the tile. The slightest side movement will damage the glazed edge of an adjacent tile that is good. If possible, remove the grout as far as the tile cement base. With a masonry bit drill a series of holes to weaken the centre of the tile, then, using a small cold chisel or a bolster, chip out the rest of the tile which should now come out quite cleanly. Remove as much of the residual tile cement so that you can bed in the new tile level with the surrounding tiles. Cleaning the space for the new tile is a delicate job requiring sensitivity and care. The reason for this is that when bedding the new tile any slight pressure on a raised point left behind will crack the new tile. Any tools used (a trimming knife is best) to scrape away residual tile cement or grout left on the sides of the four

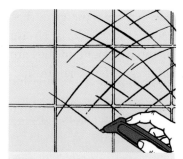

Tiling over existing tiles

If the old tiles are firmly fixed, it is possible to tile over them, providing you 'key' their surface by scoring first Remember to clean off all grease and mould. Remove silicone sealant.

adjacent tiles must be carefully used. A small scraper or a flat putty knife is good for gently smoothing the background area which can be dampened to prevent dust flying around. Before finally cementing a square tile into place have a trial run with the tile in different orientations so that you get the best fit – mark the tile with a non-permanent felt pen so that it goes in the correct way.

Regrout between tiles if the surface has suffered the effects of cooking around the stove in a kitchen, or where tiles have not been dried after a shower has been used (if the shower doors are kept closed spores can breed very easily producing a black mould). I've already described the small regrouting tool used for raking out old or perished grout. Another powered tool, used by professional tilers and DIYers alike, is a smaller version of a cordless screwdriver but with a tiny circular saw blade that cuts easily through any grout. Once you've taken the grout from the area that is to be regrouted, brush the whole area with an antifungal solution. In areas of about a square metre (square yard) liberally spread the grout and press to fill every gap and crevice in the grout joint – excess grout can go back into the container. Clean up the surface with a damp close textured sponge.

Another solution to this problem is to simply enhance the grout lines. Providing that the original grout is firm and only discoloured, use a proprietary brand of a tile renovator that comes with a sponge applicator to totally revive the grout line. Follow the instructions to get the best professional results. The process is so easy that a whole wall can be done in minutes. Simply paint on the 'grout-revive', allow to dry and then wash off. The solution is absorbed by the grout to bond with it but does not stick to glazed ceramic surfaces. An alternative is to use an applicator where a small wheel delivers the solution to the grout line.

The gap between a skirting board and the floor can widen over time. This will allow air to bring dust into a room. Use a silicone matching sealant to seal the gap and create a more attractive finish.

Cutting and marking

You must obey certain rules to ensure that you do not break a tile when scoring and snapping it. Lay the tile on a flat, clean, resilient surface. Carefully mark the exact line of the score. Use a thin straight edge (so that you can see the mark) but allow for the thickness of the end of the scoring tool. Position a piece of cable or a matchstick under the end of the scored line. Simply press on the tile to snap it.

Cutting any tiles to obtain a professional result is quick and easy with the Plasplugs protiler.

By following simple guidelines and using inexpensive tiling tools it is possible for any DIY enthusiast to carry out any of the tiling jobs previously done by a professional. There are always tiles to be shaped, but before cutting any, you first need to accurately mark them. Curved cuts at the edge of a handbasin can be carried out using a template. Fix the full tiles first of all, leaving one space for the curved cut tile. Now cut a piece of card to the exact size of the tile that is to be cut and fixed against the basin. Sometimes the card can be slid behind the basin and fitted into the space so that you can then draw an exact profile of the curve on to the card. Cut the curve on the card and transfer that to the new tile to be cut. If you can't do it this way, measure the short top line and the bottom longer line of the space and transfer those measurements to the card then cut between the two in a straight line. Force the card into the space against the vertical straight edge and crease the sloping side against the curved edge of the basin. Cut at the crease and transfer that curved cut to the new tile.

Break a quarry floor tile with a club hammer for renewing, but wear goggles.

To fit tiles around a socket outlet, you should cut them so that at least 3 mm (⅛ in) slips behind the loosened plate so that it can be tightened up to the tile surface. Again, all whole tiles must be laid and the cut tile spacers left until the last. To cut the corner out of a tile hold it in the horizontal space first and mark where the corner of the switch plate touches the tile.

Cut curves in heavy duty floor tiles to fit around the pedestal handbasin and WC. Use either a comb profiler or cut a cardboard template to transfer the shape to the tile.

Do the same for the vertical adjacent side. Measure how much the tile has to slip in both ways so that you have a matching grout line horizontally and vertically. Make these marks on the tile ready for cutting.

Fitting tiles against sloping ceilings is easier! One mark, one scribe, one cut. Hold the tile against the sloping ceiling but in line with the vertical grout lines of the already laid full tiles. Use a short wide batten as a guide. Hold the batten against the slope of the ceiling and up against the tile to be cut. This will give you the exact angle for cutting. Measure either side of the space, transfer it to the tile and make a straight angled cut.

Curved cuts

In the past, cutting curves in tiles was a tedious business. As much as possible of the waste tile was cut off after scoring straight lines, then the tiler worked up to the curved line with a nibbler or a pair of pincers. Tiny pieces were nicked out as far as the line and then a file was used to obtain a smooth curve. As more and more DIY enthusiasts began to do their own tiling, there was more demand for tools and equipment to make things easier, speedier and more economical – and so the DIY tile saw was born. This saw, similar to a junior hacksaw but slightly larger, has a long-life tungsten-

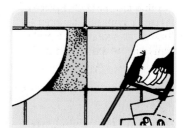

Tiling – curves

To cut a curve so that a tile fits accurately around a handbasin, make a cardboard template of the exact space to be filled and transfer the shape to the tile. A tile saw has a long-life, tungsten-coated carbide blade making it easy to cut curves. Use it to cut tiles up to 10 mm (3/8 in) thick.

coated carbide blade of circular cross-section so it cuts all around it. This makes it very easy to cut curves. The saw can even cut curves in tiles up to 10 mm (⅜ in) thick. Support the tile on the edge of a bench and cut around the curve with the tile saw. Alternatively, clamp the tile, protected with thick cardboard either side, in a vice and then carefully make the cut remembering that the saw is cutting on both the pull and the push action. Because the kerf (the slot left by the blade) is only the width of the blade, you cannot afford to tilt the blade either way. One slight movement to the left or to the right will put pressure on the brittle tile and probably break it, so take care.

Snapping tiles
Use a proprietary tool that measures, scores and snaps. This ensures that a number of tiles can be cut consistently and precisely.

Sometimes water pipes shoot out from a wall in the most inconvenient position! To cut around a pipe accurately and neatly need not be a problem. If the pipe is positioned at the edge of the tile, simply draw lines from the pipe's outer edges on to the tile with the corresponding curve in the right position. Support the tile on the edge of a bench and cut around the curve with the tile saw. If, as is more likely, the pipe position is somewhere in the centre of the tile, solve the problem by scoring the tile and snapping it at the position of the pipe centre. Draw parallel lines with the outer edges of the pipe on to both halves of the cut tile and draw corresponding curves to match the shape of the pipe. Cut both halves. When stuck in position you'll see little or no join.

Square ceramic tiles are cut so that the edges are covered by socket faceplates. The power must be switched off when working near to sockets and switches. Only restore the power when you have screwed the faceplates back into position.

An alternative method to making a cardboard template to transfer a shape to a tile is to use a 'profiler'. This brilliant device looks like a fine-toothed comb with long teeth. The polished steel teeth are held in grooves in a central bar. Each tooth slides in and out independently of the others. If you push the profiler against, for example, an architrave, the exact shape of the architrave is reproduced along the edge of the profiler. It's then a simpler matter to transfer this shape to any tile, whether it's a wall tile or a floor tile. Practically any shape can be reproduced using this ingenious device and it is an essential part of the DIYer's tiling tool box.

Straight cuts

It has long been the practice to make straight cuts on tiles by first scoring along a marked line, placing two matchsticks under the tile (one either end under the scored line), and then pressing down either side to snap the tile. Larger tiles, floor tiles and frost resistant tiles need to have something larger than a matchstick, and professional tilers often use two pieces of electrical cable, but a tile jig or a 'snapper' is best when many repeat straight cuts are needed as it makes accurate and clean cuts every time. This is because you can actually see the line and the wheel that does the scoring. The hardest part of this process is the accurate marking of the tile after measuring the space, taking into account grout lines either side of the cut tile. Place the tile on the platform underneath the scoring wheel, lower the handle and pull it so that the scoring wheel is in contact with the whole length of the tile. You can be sure that you can solve the problem of scoring exactly on the line by taking into account the thickness of the tool at the point where the spindle holds the scoring wheel. Lift the tile into the jaws of the 'snapper', press down on the handle and you get a straight accurate cut. Always smooth the sharp edge of any cut tile with sandpaper or even with a nail file.

If you have a gentle curve to snap, say, up to 25 mm (1 in) out of a true straight line, you can still do this by putting matchsticks under each end of the scored line and gently pressing down either side. This will snap the tile exactly where you want but only if you continue the scored line to either side of the tile.

To successfully snap quarry tiles, the scored line must be strong and continuous from the one edge to the opposite edge. With a lightweight hammer tap the back of the tile along the line of the score until you get a clean break. Contemporary quarry tiles are 150 mm (6 in) square and so they can be comfortably held in the left hand whilst tapping its back until it snaps. Obviously wear gloves to protect your hands. The secret to a clean cut, especially on a floor tile, is to have a scoring tool with a high-quality wheel. Tools are available that have the capacity to successfully score ceramic wall tiles, quarry tiles, frostproof floor tiles, laminates, glass and mirrors. It is recommended that every time you use these tools that you add a little oil to the wheel. This not only stops the wheel jamming but also aids the scoring process.

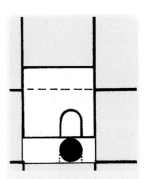

Cutting a wall tile to fit around a socket or switch (1)

Hold the tile against the socket and mark the cuts allowing 3 mm (1/8 in) to go under the faceplate. Make the shortest cut with a tile saw.

Cutting a wall tile to fit around a socket or switch (2)

Score the tile along the longest cut mark. Use a simple tile snapper to remove the corner piece. Switch off the mains, loosen the cover plate and slip the cut tile under the edge. Gently bed it into the tile cement.

Cutting a wall tile to fit around a pipe

Hold the tile in line with the fixed tiles. Mark the outer edges and cut with a tile saw to the marked depth and to the circular shape.

Holes

Often it is necessary to drill into a wall tile or a floor tile either before or after fixing. For example, you might need to run a cable under a conservatory floor that you're going to tile. If you then go to screw a fitting to the tiled floor, say a lampholder, a water feature or a fish tank, you'll need to drill into the last tile where the cable appears. A variable speed drill is best with a tile spade bit running at a slow speed. Drill, again at slow speed, a pilot hole with a small diameter masonry bit then go to the size of bit that is required for the plug and the screw to hold the fitting. There are special bits available for drilling holes into frostproof tiles. These will literally drill into any building material, heavy gauge metal and even glass bottles!

Before you drill holes in ceramic wall tiles for hanging mirrors, wall cupboards or pictures, be certain that you know what the wall material is and then for your own safety, check with a cable and pipe detector that where you're drilling is safe. These are inexpensive and can save you a great deal of time and money. Remember – SAFETY FIRST, DIY SECOND. You might drill into a water pipe which will obviously cause a great deal of hassle and damage. This actually happened to former tennis star Annabel Croft. As a keen DIYer she was helping in the preparatory work for a 'make-over' in one of the rooms at her home. She knew the procedure for drilling through tiles, but not for checking for pipes and cables before drilling. She drilled into a water pipe with dire consequences which could have been worse had she not known where the stopcock was.

Manufacturers are now much more aware of the needs of DIYers and are designing and developing DIY tools with features only previously enjoyed by the tradesman. For example, Draper has produced an inexpensive diamond-wheel tile-cutter which is foolproof, easy to use and produces an accurate straight cut every time.

Another manufacturer with a similar outlook is Harris and their 'No Loss' brush – a new concept in quality paint brushes that loose no bristles and give a smoother finish.

International Paints have successfully developed a paint that actually covers melamine surfaces and a radiator paint that tolerates the build up of heat. This, after producing an innovative anti-condensation paint that helps prevent damp on vulnerable walls.

Before decorating a bathroom or kitchen, consider a decorative finish of tongue and groove boards up to dado rail height, or you may totally cover walls (or a ceiling) in panelling.

The very best tool for this job is the Rapesco 191 Nail/Staple gun. Previously this remarkable tool was used by professionals, but it's now designed and developed with the DIYer in mind.

For a completely new look to a room, consider a technique that you've admired elsewhere but have baulked at doing it yourself! For example, check the many effects that you can achieve with Artex and its complementary tools. You'll be amazed by the incredible range.

A last thought – buy the best, but not necessarily the most expensive. There is no substitute for quality. Paul McKenna liked my choice of H&R Johnson tiles when I tiled his kitchen. And he helped, but not hypnotically, just by using the tools that I write about!

Index